THE
creative
lapidary

MATERIALS
TOOLS
TECHNIQUES
DESIGN

FRANK W. LONG

 VAN NOSTRAND REINHOLD COMPANY
New York   Cincinnati   Toronto   London   Melbourne

This book is dedicated to the many fine craftsmen who constantly strive to express the highest possible creative excellence in their work.

TS
752.5
L65

Copyright © 1976 by Litton Educational Publishing, Inc.
Library of Congress Catalog Card Number 76-21357
ISBN 0-442-24887-3

Printed in the United States of America
Designed by Loudan Enterprises

Published in 1976 by Van Nostrand Reinhold Company
A Division of Litton Educational Publishing, Inc.
450 West 33rd Street
New York, NY 10001

Van Nostrand Reinhold Limited
1410 Birchmount Road
Scarborough, Ontario M1P 2E7, Canada

Van Nostrand Reinhold Australia Pty. Ltd.
17 Queen Street
Mitcham, Victoria 3132, Australia

Van Nostrand Reinhold Company Ltd.
Molly Millars Lane
Wokingham, Berkshire, England

16 15 14 13 12 11 10 9 8 7 6 5 4 3 2 1

Library of Congress Cataloging in Publication Data

Long, Frank W
   The creative lapidary.

   Bibliography: p.
   Includes index.
   1. Gem cutting.   I. Title.
TS752.5.L65   736'.2'028   76-21357
ISBN 0-442-24887-3

Photo Credits

The following illustrations are reproduced by the courtesy of the sources named:

1-2, 1-3, 4-2, 4-32, 5-44 photos by Dick Dunatchik

1-8 Institute of Geological Sciences, London

2-3, 2-9, 2-18, 2-19, 2-21, 2-24, 2-26, 2-27, 2-28, 2-29, 2-31, 2-36, 2-54 Highland Park Manufacturing; photos by W. Roy Watson

2-4, 2-23 Alta Industries

2-5 Great Western Equipment Company

2-6, 2-14, 2-30 Crown Manufacturing Company

2-7, 2-22, 2-32, 2-56, 2-58, 2-59 Covington Engineering Corp.

2-8 A. D. McBurney

2-11, 2-15 Brad's Rock Shop

2-20 Diamond Pacific Tool Corp.

2-22, 2-32, 4-29, 4-37, 5-11, 5-24, 5-40, 5-54, 6-11 photos by Wilbur Henry

2-34, 2-57 Lortone, Incorporated

2-35 Vibra-Tek

2-37 Vitromet Diamond Tool Company

2-41, 2-44, Paul H. Gesswein and Company, Inc.

2-42 Dremel Manufacturing Company

2-51 M.D.R. Manufacturing Company, Inc.; photo by Meriman Photography Co., Inc.

2-52 Dick Blick, photo by Dick Dunatchik

4-4, 4-26, 4-28, 4-30, 4-34, 4-35, 5-7, 5-8, 5-12, 5-16, 5-19, 5-20, 5-21, 5-41, 6-2, C-1, C-11, C-17 U.S. Department of the Interior, Indian Arts and Crafts Board

4-20 photo by the author

5-1, 5-2, 5-3 Field Museum of Natural History

5-4 Dr. James Robert Moriarty, III

5-5, 5-6 Museum of the American Indian, Heye Foundation

5-10, 5-14, 6-1 American Crafts Council; photos by Ferdinand Boesch

5-49 Kraft Foods

5-50, C-21 photos by Country Studio

5-52 photo by Woltz Studio

6-5 photo by Tom Yee

6-6, 6-9, 6-13 Museum of Contemporary Crafts, American Crafts Council

Acknowledgments

The author's warm gratitude is extended to his friends who have so generously given their assistance to the writing of this book. The following deserve special mention: Vinita Hopkins, Bette Casteel, George Tennant, Jo Cockelreas, Wilbur Henry, Ruth Schultz, and Phyllis Hersh. Warmest thanks to Harry Mefford for his unfailing faith and encouragement. The author also wishes to acknowledge the substantial assistance of the American Crafts Council and of the Indian Arts and Crafts Board, United States Department of the Interior.

In the many years of study and experimentation that resulted in this book, numerous sources were consulted. Particularly helpful were *The Art of the Lapidary* by Francis J. Sperisen and *How to Make and Use Gem Carving Tools* by Forrest W. Pond.

Drawings, photographs, and lapidary works not specifically credited to others are by the author.

Contents

Preface

The art of lapidary is in a curious state. More people are engaged in it than at any time in the past; more gems are produced and used in jewelry; more lapidary equipment is bought and sold; more is written and published on the subject than ever before. It is the third largest and fastest-growing of all hobbies. Few cities of any size in the United States do not have at least one lapidary or gem-and-mineral club. There is also a national federation of lapidary organizations. But in spite of this flood of activity and enthusiasm the craft is artistically dead! No doubt this statement will be heatedly disputed by many people, but the truth remains that today's lapidary work has no creative significance. It has no relation to the contemporary crafts movement, which is rapidly making itself felt as a new force in modern art.

The fact is that "serious" craftsmen—those who pursue their work professionally as an art form—have shown practically no interest in the lapidary medium. This seems very strange in view of the experimental and exploratory approach toward materials and techniques that is basic to the new movement. It is particularly inconsistent in the case of designer-jewelers, most of whom seem content to incorporate in their work commercially produced stones with standardized shapes and cuts that have varied little in the last 200 years. Still more surprising is the apparent lack of awareness of the many possible applications and innovations offered by the medium in other fields. This might not be so hard to understand were it not for the impressive lapidary work of the ancient Egyptians, the pre-Columbian cultures of the Americas, and the Chinese throughout their long history. Examples of this work are familiar to every culturally educated person. It would appear that such examples would inevitably suggest possibilities for contemporary styles and applications and for the creation of totally new concepts and uses as well.

There are factors that may explain why modern craftsmen have neglected this fertile field and shown no interest in what it might produce if properly cultivated. The reason is at least partly traditional: lapidaries have always been specialists, producing their work for the use of jewelers and other craftsmen. Long before the industrial revolution the gem industry had developed in Europe as separate and distinct from the jewelry industry. In America, carrying on the European tradition, commercial gemstones are calibrated on the metric system to fit settings manufactures to the same scale. They are cut by skilled technicians who rigidly follow standardized patterns developed long ago. Today's designer-jewelers, who pursue their craft as a means of artistic expression, seem unaware that this highly restrictive and creatively illogical situation needs changing and that they are the only people who can change it.

The author does not mean to imply that the whole world of crafts is totally insensitive to this state of affairs or that he is the only craftsman who is aware of the inconsistency. A few outstanding designer-jewelers—the late Margaret de Patta and Irena Brynner, for example—have arranged on occasion for lapidaries such as Francis J. Sperisen to produce stones to fit their designs and were thus able to create conceptions of greater consistency and originality. Perhaps others unknown to the author have worked out similar cooperative arrangements. Such collaboration should be fostered and encouraged. From the creative standpoint it is vastly preferable to a continued dependency on the prefabricated stones offered by the market. But it must be realized that any significant improvement of the situation, any artistic development of the craft, will have to be made by talented designers who work directly in the medium. A full understanding of the possibilities and limitations of any craft can be gained only from actual practice and experimentation.

Despite a growing appreciation and acceptance of the creative significance of crafts, a climate in which lapidary can flourish on an equal plane with other media has not evolved. In addition to the traditional false position it has occupied, other factors work against its development. The fact that the craft, except for the commercial lapidaries, is in the hands of amateurs and hobbyists has undoubtedly discouraged the interest of professional designer-craftsmen. Although the work of many amateurs reveals great technical skill and even a high degree of artistic talent, it shows little awareness of contemporary aesthetic values and directions in design. This is not surprising, since most amateurs and hobbyists have little background or professional training in the arts. What is disappointing is the fact that the professionals, who have this understanding, have shown no interest in the possibilities of developing the craft on a higher level.

This apathy is reflected and perpetuated in art education. Since there are no practitioners in the lapidary field academically qualified to teach on the college level, it is not surprising that lapidary classes are not offered at any major art schools or universities in the country. The situation is also perpetuated by the major crafts exhibitions, many of which are promoted and controlled by these institutions. These shows make no provision for recognizing lapidary work as a legitimate medium. (Oddly, it is only some of the smaller exhibitions that include a "miscellaneous" category in which work not done in any of the standard media can be entered.) Furthermore, although entries in competitive shows are normally required to be entirely the work of the exhibitor, no jury hesitates to accept jewelry in which the stones are obviously of commercial origin. It appears to be the rather vague assumption of judges and craftsmen alike that the lapidary craft is arcane, esoteric, mechanical—an appropriate field for artisan specialists but no place for the creative craftsman.

In the author's opinion these are the principal reasons why the art of lapidary is languishing today. No one is responsible for the situation: it has developed gradually, insidiously, over a long period of time. Not until the present has there appeared to be any reason to question the status quo. But now that crafts are expressing contemporary aesthetics, challenging tradition, seeking new approaches, investigating every possible material and technique, the time is ripe for the craft world to take a closer look at the inspiring art of the lapidary.

There are many fine books on lapidary materials and techniques, so many in fact that another might seem superfluous. But the author feels that there is an urgent need for a book that reveals the possibilities of the craft as a contemporary creative medium, something that no other book has attempted. It is hoped that among today's many talented designer-craftsmen some will find here an incentive to investigate the possibilities for themselves. In no other way will the craft ever be significantly developed.

But this book is not written with only such craftsmen in mind. The art of lapidary is a wide-open field that offers unrestricted opportunities to professionals and amateurs alike. Among the vast numbers of amateurs and hobbyists there is abundant evidence that much latent creative ability exists. Perhaps it needs only to be awakened to more stimulating approaches in order to evolve away from the uninspiring kind of work that unfortunately characterizes most of what is being done today. Someone working purely for recreation or relaxation must still be satisfied with the results. True satisfaction is attained only if one succeeds in being and expressing oneself. Every individual needs only the proper stimulus to start discovering his creative identity in the work that he does—a new direction, a new awareness of the higher values within his reach. It is hoped that at least some will find such a stimulus in this book.

A note about the word "creative": it is an overused, misused, much abused term. It has become an annoying habit of the general public to apply it to almost anything with artistic pretensions. It is used so indiscriminately in this connection that one is tempted to try to avoid it altogether in discussing any kind of art. Unfortunately there is no substitute for its strict meaning: originality of thought or expression. It is in this sense that it is used in this book, always with the hope that it will not be misunderstood.

1. Materials

There is ample evidence that man has always been fascinated by the rocks and minerals of the earth. Recently he has become even more intrigued with those of the moon. No doubt this fascination will be extended to the materials of the planets and other astral bodies of outer space as man concentrates his scientific skills on an effort to understand the origin and composition of the universe. But those of us who are not scientists respond more subjectively to the earth's materials, particularly to the gem materials. They capture our imagination with their crystalline facets, their limpidity, their brilliant and varied colors and patterns, their absorption and reflection of light, the mystery and wonder of their creation. This response appears to be fundamental. Even certain birds and mammals gather brightly colored pebbles for no discernible reason other than fascination with their appearance. Small wonder that collecting, studying, and working with these materials has preoccupied man through the ages and today engages the attention of such large numbers of people.

To find a bit of stone formed in the recesses of the earth thousands to millions of years ago, to shape it and polish it so that its inner beauty comes to light, is an adventure that puts one in touch with the infinite. To go still further and form it into an object that expresses a personal response to its unique qualities in an original aesthetic statement is to experience the ultimate thrill of creation.

Durable, beautiful, and rare—these are the most sought-after qualities in a material, particularly by those who make it into a precious object. Althouth there is a trend in contemporary art away from calculated permanence, most people have a basic, often unconscious respect for the durable and the immutable. This is particularly true for objects whose beauty excites our admiration;

the effect is heightened if we feel that the object will endure. The rarity of a material makes it more desirable because most people have a psychological preference for the unusual over the commonplace.

After weapons and tools the first use of hard, durable materials was possibly for jewelry. It seems reasonable to conjecture that the first example of jewelry was a piece of stone, shell, or bone with a natural hole that was strung on a thong and hung around the neck of Paleolithic man. From this first step, which must have produced a profound effect on all who beheld it, piercing fragments of attractive materials to make personal adornments followed naturally though by no means quickly. Many centuries of painful effort and experiment intervened before the first crude drill was invented. And another very long period separated the development of drills that would pierce the softer materials and those used to drill hard stone successfully.

The prehistoric lapidary preceded the first metalsmith by many thousands of years. Until ways to work metal were discovered, stone was the only material available from which efficient tools and weapons could be made. The consummate skill with which these were fashioned during Neolithic periods never ceases to amaze both anthropologists and craftsmen. There is mute evidence also of an awakening aesthetic sense in the so-called laurel-leaf points and blades made by the Solutrean culture of 17,000 to 20,000 years ago. Some of these are so fragile that they would have been useless for any practical purpose: they could only have been made as a demonstration of skill, of respect for the material, and of a sensitivity to beauty of form. These incentives remain the strongest motivation of lapidaries today.

Once the basic techniques of melting, casting, and alloying were mastered, metalwork developed more rapidly than the more difficult stoneworking techniques. Metal was softer, less rigid and unyielding, hence more easily formed into a wide variety of useful shapes. But it lacked the imagination-stirring attributes of the gem minerals, and, although during the Bronze Age metal tools, utensils, and weapons quickly replaced those of stone, in most cultures in which both were available gemstones and gem materials were valued more highly for artistic purposes. According to Montezuma's scale of values among the Aztecs jade, turquoise, quetzal plumes, and gold, respectively, were the most prized materials. The Chinese also placed jade, along with several other stones, above gold as a precious material. The ancient Egyptians were equally appreciative of the gem minerals and used them lavishly, both alone and in combination with metals.

When metal coins began to be used as a medium of exchange, a new system of evaluation was introduced in which metals were basic. Everything began to be appraised on a monetary basis, and the value of gem materials has since been based on cost rather than an aesthetic appeal.

Cost is determined primarily by the durability, rarity, and popularity of a material. To a much lesser degree it

1-1. Eskimo tools: (1) skin scraper, jade bit, wood handle; (2) adze, jade bit, caribou-horn handle and socket.

is affected by beauty. The diamond, the most popular stone, best illustrates the point. It is the hardest, most durable of stones, but if it were available at $1 a carat, it would lose its popularity overnight. The only reason why one diamond costs twice as much as another that looks exactly like it to the naked eye is because under magnification the former is perfect, while the latter has tiny flaws. A perfect diamond is relatively rare. As far as beauty is concerned, some glass imitations disperse the spectrum colors far more brilliantly. But even a perfect diamond is not the costliest stone: perfect emeralds and rubies bring higher prices carat for carat. This is because they are more rare, not because they are more beautiful or more popular.

In spite of the false values created by materialist civilizations, people have retained their sense of wonder and delight in earth's natural phenomena. As long as this holds true, no matter what the economic situation, gems and minerals will never cease to fascinate and to be sought after for their own sake. And as long as aesthetic perception and creative ability are attributes of the human mind, gem materials will continue to be used to create objects of beauty.

Types of Materials
The modern lapidary has at his disposal a greater variety of gem materials than was available in any past period. New materials are still being discovered and added to the long list. More than two hundred materials are commonly used for decorative purposes. The creative artist has at his command a full spectrum of color values, and there are many variations of opacity, translucency, transparency, texture, and pattern and a great range in the refraction, dispersion, and diffusion of light. All of these qualities offer aesthetic possibilities to the creative lapidary.

By strict definition a lapidary (lapidist and lapidarist are recently introduced synonyms) is a person who cuts, grinds, and polishes precious stones. But what are precious stones? Again by strict definition they are limited to the diamond, ruby, sapphire, and emerald. But if monetary value is the basis, others should be included: fine opals and fine jade can be just as "precious" as those listed. However, the lapidary is not limited to specific stones: he may utilize all that are commonly worked and many that are not, including semiprecious and ornamental materials. The latter are generally used for carvings or decorative work rather than for jewelry. A more accurate definition of a lapidary might be a person who cuts, grinds, and polishes gemstones or other materials for a variety of purposes.

Classification of Materials

Most of the materials used by the lapidary are minerals that come from the earth. Others (*synthetics*) are created by man to duplicate or simulate natural minerals; others (*organic materials*) are not minerals at all. One often hears the joint term "rocks and minerals." The two classifications are usually treated together in works on geology and mineralogy. What is the difference? Both are mineral in nature. A *mineral* is either a basic element, designated by a chemical symbol, or a compound, expressed by a chemical formula. For instance, the symbol for aluminum is Al, and the formula for corundum (ruby and sapphire) is Al_2O_3: two atoms of aluminum and three of oxygen. A *rock*, on the other hand, is an aggregate of many different particles of various minerals. Marble, one of the simpler rocks, is an aggregate of calcite, $CaCO_3$, and quartzite, SiO_2. Generally speaking, rocks are softer, less compact, and hard to polish. For this reason most rocks have comparatively little eye appeal for decorative work and are seldom used by lapidaries.

Gem materials are listed under two broad classifications: *organic* and *inorganic*. Materials of organic origin are comparatively few in number; examples are ivory, bone, hoof, horn, wood, jet, coal, coral, shell, pearl, amber, baleen (whalebone), gorgonian (a sea plant), and vegetable ivory (1-2).

Inorganic materials (1-3) are divided into three groups: *crystalline*, *cryptocrystalline*, and *amorphous*. Crystalline minerals exhibit crystal forms that are visible without high-power magnification. Cryptocrystalline materials are composed of crystals so small they cannot be seen without such assistance. Some minerals exhibit both forms. The quartz family is a common example: amethyst is a crystalline form and agate is cryptocrystalline. The crystal structure of both is identical except for size. Amorphous minerals, such as opal, lack any discernible crystal structure.

Any lapidary who does an appreciable variety of work can be expected to use metals such as copper, silver, and gold in combination with stones. As mentioned previously, metals in their elemental form have quite different characteristics from the gem materials. To use them in this state or alloyed with other metals, a knowledge of metalcraft techniques is required. They are normally used by the lapidary to create a framework or an embellishment for gems or other stonework. Some of the metallic ores, however, are compounds that can be ground and polished in the same manner as other gem minerals. Hematite (Fe_2O_3), a very pure iron ore, is one example. The so-called black diamonds are faceted from this material. Other metallic ores show

striking forms that the imaginative craftsman may wish to utilize in an unaltered state, just as he may sometimes wish to use other natural crystals without appreciably changing their shape.

It is beyond the scope of this book to deal other than peripherally with crystallography and the classification and identification of gems. Intriguing as these specialties may be, they are more important to the mineralogist and the gemologist, the gem dealer and the commercial jeweler than to the creative craftsman. The lapidary-jeweler does need to know the characteristics of the materials he employs and should be able to use the terminology correctly. He should know the relative hardness of materials and their tendency to split, or cleave, in certain directions. The serious craftsman should learn as much as possible of a practical nature about the materials with which he works.

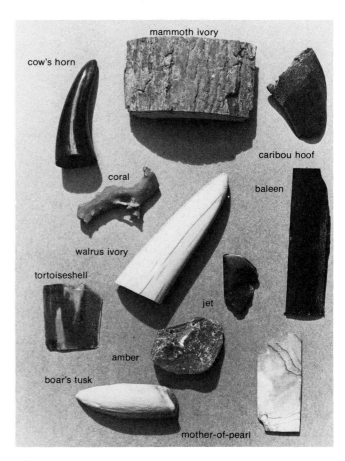

1-2.

10

tigereye

peridot

sunstone

nephrite

fluorite

rose quartz

iron pyrite

quartz crystal

turquoise

hematite

ruby

pink tourmaline

moonstone

lapis lazuli

aquamarine

opal

agate

carnelian

malachite

kunzite

topaz

amethyst

1-3.

11

There are some fairly simple tests for identifying most lapidary materials. They will serve in the majority of cases. Often several tests are required for positive identification. If all should fail and identification is vital, a mineralogist or a gemologist should be consulted. These specialists have the technical knowledge and the special equipment required for complete analysis. Once the principal characteristics of a material have been ascertained by testing, its identity can be established by referring to a mineralogy book that gives a complete descriptive list of minerals. These reference works provide information on the chemical content, crystal structure, specific gravity, hardness, cleavage, fracture, luster, and color of mineral materials.

Minerals can be classified according to which of six *crystal systems* (1-4) they belong: *triclinic, isometric, hexagonal, tetragonal, orthorhombic,* and *monoclinic.* These terms designate the different angles and proportions of imaginary internal axes; they do not necessarily indicate the external forms, although ratios between the interfacial angles remain constant for a given mineral species. This fact can be useful as a fairly simple means of mineral identification. If a specimen is large enough, a simple, inexpensive instrument called a *contact goniometer* (1-5) can be used to measure the angles. Tables on crystallography that list the interfacial angles for each mineral can then be referred to for identification.

1-4.

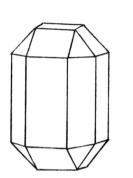

orthorhombic (chrysolite)

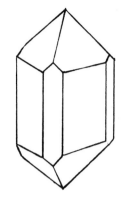

monoclinic (jadeite)

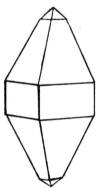

tetragonal (zircon)

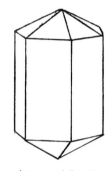

hexagonal (beryl)

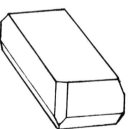

triclinic (rhodonite)

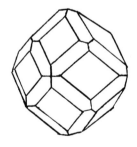

isometric (garnet)

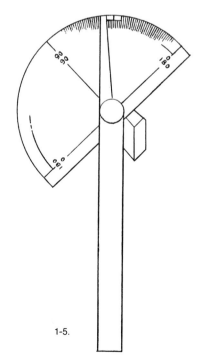

1-5.

Specific gravity refers to the weight of a substance in comparison to an equal volume of water. It can also be used by the lapidary for identification purposes. The mineralogist may use any one of several scales for this purpose, all fairly expensive. They are constructed in such a way that the specimen can be weighed first in air, then in water. It is not practical for the craftsman to invest in such equipment, since he may have only occasional use for it. A certain type of gold scale (1-6) can be adapted very easily to measure specific gravity by making a small tripod platform to set above one of the balance pans. The platform is used to hold a small container of water, and the specimen is fastened to the arm above the container by means of a fine wire so that it is suspended in the water and balanced with weights in the pan on the other arm. The pan must swing free of the platform, and the specimen should not touch the sides of the container. The wire used to suspend the piece must be weighed and the result subtracted from the total weight, and air bubbles on the wire or the specimen must be dispersed. The specimen is then weighed in the regular way, in air. The specific gravity is obtained with the following formula:

$$\text{specific gravity} = \frac{\text{weight in air}}{\text{weight in air} - \text{weight in water}}$$

For large specimens the displacement method is used. A container fitted with an outlet (1-7) is filled with water to the bottom of the outlet. The specimen is then placed in the water, and the water it displaces is caught in a dry container. The weight of the drawn-off water is obtained by deducting the weight of the container when dry from its weight with the water. The specific gravity is then calculated as follows:

$$\text{specific gravity} = \frac{\text{weight of specimen in air}}{\text{weight of water displaced}}$$

One of the most important characteristics of gem materials for lapidary purposes is *hardness*. It is essential to know whether or not a given material is hard enough, for the intended use. Stones for rings must be hard enough to withstand shocks and abrasion; stones for pins, necklaces, and earrings can be less resistant to wear. A knowledge of relative hardness is very useful in setting stones, because tools such as gravers and files must be used with great care if the material is softer than the steel of these tools.

The best-known hardness scale for minerals is the *Mohs' scale*, named for its inventor, Friedrich Mohs. It is the standard used in mineralogical tables. The scale lists a group of common minerals as follows:

1. talc
2. gypsum
3. calcite
4. fluorite
5. apatite
6. feldspar
7. quartz
8. topaz
9. corundum
10. diamond

1-6.

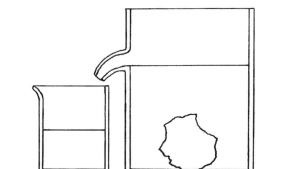

1-7.

Working from 10 downward—diamond is the hardest substance—each material will scratch the next in line. A set of hardness points made of these materials, obtainable at lapidary-supply houses, may be used to determine a mineral's relative hardness by the scratch test. There is no problem in applying the test to rough materials, but it must be used with caution on finished stones. Most faceted stones are left with a narrow unpolished girdle, which can be scratched without damaging the appearance or the value of the gem. Other cuts such as cabochons should be tested with a tiny scratch in an inconspicuous spot on the back, then repolished at that point if necessary.

Although the Mohs' scale is in universal use, it is imprecise and can be misleading if accepted without qualification. The natural assumption is that the steps are fairly equally divided, but this is not the case. Diamond is at least ten times as hard as corundum; corundum is about six times as hard as topaz; topaz is roughly twice as hard as quartz. Many minerals fall in between the steps of the scale. In such cases the common practice is to use decimals to show quarter steps. It is useful to know that a knife blade rates about 5.50, and a file and graver about 6.50. Appendix 1 gives the Mohs'-scale hardness of most lapidary materials. There are more extensive lists in mineralogy and gemology books.

Toughness is the ability of a material to resist shock, strain, or pressure. This is a different quality from hardness. Some relatively hard materials are quite fragile. They chip or fracture easily and require care in working and mounting. Other softer materials may resist breakage or chipping and for this reason are ideal for carving and for use in thin sections. Nephrite jade is the outstanding example of a tough material.

Color is one of the most attractive qualities of gem materials. It can also offer helpful clues in identification, although it cannot be relied upon completely since several materials have the same coloration—for example, topaz and citrine quartz. Many synthetics successfully duplicate the colors of the gems they simulate.

Few gems are uniformly colored throughout. In some transparent stones, notably amethyst, the color often appears in thin patches or layers surrounded by colorless material. Such stones must be oriented carefully in cutting so that the areas of color parallel the table, or top, of the stone. The colorless areas will not be seen, and the whole gem will appear uniform in color. Very translucent materials that are weak in color can be intensified by cutting a fairly thick stone. Conversely, stones that have strong color but are more opaque can be intensified by cutting a thin gem.

Fracture and *cleavage* represent the manner in which materials break under strain, pressure, or shock. Many minerals have definite cleavage planes, determined by their crystalline structure; others have none. Some cleave, or split, very easily along the cleavage planes; others have greater tenacity. Knowing the angle and degree of resistance to cleavage can be very important in orienting some stones for cutting. A stone that cleaves easily is less likely to split if the cleavage planes are kept parallel to the horizontal rather than to the vertical axis of the finished stone.

Fracture is different from cleavage. It refers to breaks in directions other than along the cleavage planes. A material may have both cleavage and fracture. Cleavage angles and fracture characteristics are given in mineralogical tables. Both can be used in identification. For example, quartz-family minerals have a typical conchoidal fracture (shaped like a shell), and labradorite has distinct cleavage in two directions, which are almost 90° to each other.

Luster in gem materials refers to the manner in which light is reflected from the surface. This is affected by the *refractive index* of each mineral: the higher the index number, the greater the luster. Diamond, zircon, and other materials with an index of 1.90 or above exhibit *adamantine* luster. Stones with an index between 1.75 and 1.90 show *subadamantine* luster. More descriptive terms are used for the luster of other materials with lower indexes, such as *resinous* for amber, *pearly* for pearls and mother-of-pearl, *waxy* for turquoise, and *vitreous* for quartz and other silicates.

Closely akin to luster are various optical phenomena caused by the reflection of light from inclusions or structural peculiarities within the stone. Some fibrous materials possess *chatoyancy* due to the reflection of light from fibrous crystals lying parallel to each other on certain planes. This results in a light that seems to move as the stone changes position, somewhat like the reflecton of light in the eye of a cat, and some stones showing this peculiarity are called *cat's-eyes*. Chrysoberyl cat's-eye and tigereye (quartz) are two examples. Nephrite jade occasionally shows this effect, as do several other materials (1-8).

Similar to chatoyancy are the effects known as *schiller*, as in sunstone; *opalescence*, as in moonstone; and *iridescence*, as in one type of obsidian and in fire agate. Most feldspars show some such effect. Labradorite is one of these, and its brilliant play of color has become known as *labradorescence*.

Asterism, which is attributable to a special arrangement of inclusions, results in rays that emanate from

1-8.

the center of a stone cut with a high, rounded crown. These are the *star* stones, such as star ruby, star sapphire, and star garnet. Synthetic star rubies and sapphires have been produced, but because of their unvarying perfection they are not difficult to distinguish from natural stones.

Paradoxically, opals that exhibit strong play of brilliant colors are not opalescent. As mentioned above, opalescence characterizes moonstones, which shows a sort of light within a milky transparency. The term originated from the so-called water opal. There is no special term for the play of prismatic color seen only in what today is called *fire opal*, traditionally a solid red color now often called cherry opal. It can be faceted effectively to reflect light through the body color. The brilliant display of color found in fire opals is caused by microscopic fissures in this amorphous material, which reflect the spectrum in myriad hues as the stone is turned in the light. Base colors in which the fire occurs may be white, black, gray, blue, green, violet, yellow—indeed, almost any color. The pattern of the fire may be called *flash*, *pinpoint*, or *harlequin*, according

to its form. The opal is the only valuable stone that has not been successfully imitated.

Gemstone materials have many varying characteristics that are important for the lapidary to be aware of. Although it is not necessary for the craftsman to delve deeply into the subject of mineralogy, if he expects to work effectively and to make the most creative use of his materials, he must understand their properties and working qualities. There is no substitute for empirical knowledge, but a study of basic information is a good investment. Only a brief summary is presented here. Further information can be obtained from the specialized works listed in the bibliography.

Sources of Materials

Raw, or *rough*, materials can be obtained from any of the numerous dealers who specialize in gemstones. Many of these advertise in the major lapidary magazines. These ads offer vivid descriptions of alluring materials, but be careful: it is safest to order only from dealers who offer a money-back guarantee on materials returned in unaltered condition within 10 days. Most dealers are honest and anxious to please their patrons. The beginner is usually surprised to discover how inexpensive most rough materials are in comparison with finished gems. This is just one of the many advantages of cutting one's own stones.

Another intriguing possibility is to look for raw materials in their natural locations. Most states have at least some workable deposits, and those who are so inclined may find it pleasurable to prospect for their own materials. In many of the western states a considerable variety of usable if not valuable materials can be found without a vast amount of effort. Many varieties of quartz are available—agate, chalcedony, petrified wood, and jasper, for example. Many deposits are in the public domain, and, if mineral claims have not been staked, any individual may prospect. Much of the material occurs as *float* and can be picked up without digging. Much good material is on private land. Some landowners do not object to prospecting; others charge a small fee; but one should always obtain permission beforehand. There are laws restricting the amount of some materials that can be removed from public lands: petrified wood is now so protected. These laws, landowners' attitudes, and local conditions should always be checked carefully. And don't forget to look out for bulls and rattlesnakes! Articles on the location of various deposits are periodically published in lapidary magazines, and handbook guides to many of these locations are available (see the bibliography).

2. Tools and Equipment

One of the commonest misconceptions about lapidary work is that it requires elaborate and expensive equipment. While a competely equipped shop can cost several thousand dollars, it is also possible to dispense with mechanical equipment entirely and achieve excellent results by hand with an outlay of only a few dollars for materials (see chapter 4 on hand cutting). The range of work that can be done by hand is limited and time-consuming, but simple, professional-quality stones can be produced.

How much equipment you need depends on the type of work that you want to do and on whether you are an amateur, with lots of time but little money to spend, or a professional, who depends on sales for his income. If you are an amateur, you may need only the minimum that will enable you to produce your best work, even though it may be slower than with more elaborate equipment. But if you are a professional, time is money; time-saving equipment will soon be paid for by the greater profit per hour that you will make. In either case it is common sense to begin with the most basic equipment and add to it as the need develops.

No one should be discouraged by the cost factor. Many amateurs and professionals have been able to cut costs materially by either making most of their equipment from scratch or assembling it from manufactured or improvised parts. Ingenuity and some mechanical ability are required, and the time factor will determine just how practical this effort is in a particular case. In the last section of this chapter instructions are given for constructing homemade equipment.

Lapidary equipment can be divided into several general categories: saws, grinders, sanders, polishers, drills, carvers, laps, faceters, and tumblers. There are several different types of each, as well as a number of attachments, mechanical aids, and hand tools that can be helpful. Unfortunately, there are also some doubtful products on the market. In fact, because of the tremendous interest in lapidary work there is such a bewildering array of different brands and models that the beginner may find it difficult to select equipment intelligently without some guidance. This chapter tries to help by describing what the author considers to be the best *types* of equipment for various kinds of work. Most of the recommendations are made on the basis of personal experience; in some cases other sources have been consulted. Specific *brand names* are avoided if quality and performance are approximately equal. If possible, consult an experienced lapidary before setting up your shop. He can give valuable information on the relative quality and performance of various brands. In general, well-established manufacturers can be relied upon for quality products, although some lesser-known brands are reliable and lower in cost. The important considerations are good mechanical design and high-quality materials and workmanship.

Saws

Lapidary saws are used for three different kinds of cutting: sectioning, slabbing, and trimming.

Sectioning saws are primarily used to divide large masses of stone into blocks that can be cut by smaller slabbing saws. Some are portable and can be operated in the field where large gem boulders are found. There are three types of sectioning saws: *straight-blade*, *circular-blade*, and *continuous-blade*. The first is designed on the same principle as the power-driven hacksaws used to cut metal; the second is simply a large circular saw; the third consists of a twisted wire that travels over large pulleys. Chinese craftsmen used a sectioning saw that also had a twisted-wire blade. An abrasive mixture was fed to the cut while two men pulled the wire, mounted in a saw frame, back and forth across the stone (2-1). Most lapidaries do not use large sectioning saws. Slabbing and trim saws are standard equipment in the individual lapidary shop.

Slabbing saws (2-2 and 2-3), as the name indicates, are used to saw slabs of predetermined thickness from blocks or rough masses of medium-size material. The dimensions of material that can be sawed are determined by the size of the blade and the size of the vise. The blade can vary from 10" to 36" in diameter; the vise, from a few inches to over 2' capacity.

The *shaft*, usually called an *arbor* or *mandrel*, should run on sealed ball bearings for long, troublefree use. It should be large enough in diameter to remain rigid during operation: 5/8" is the minimum diameter for 10" to 16" blades; 3/4" to 1 1/2", for blades up to 36" in diameter.

The flanges that flank the blade should be accurately machined and large enough in diameter to support the blade firmly. Thin blades need wider support than thicker ones. If blades of different thicknesses are used on the same machine, be sure that the flanges are large enough for the thinnest blade. Consult the manufacturer's recommendations.

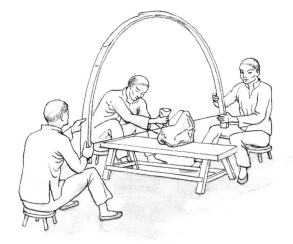

2-1.

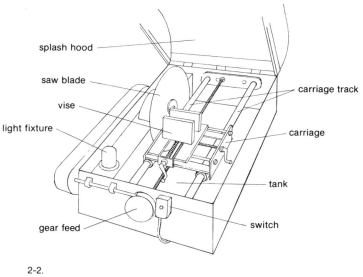

splash hood

saw blade

vise

light fixture

carriage track

carriage

tank

gear feed

switch

2-2.

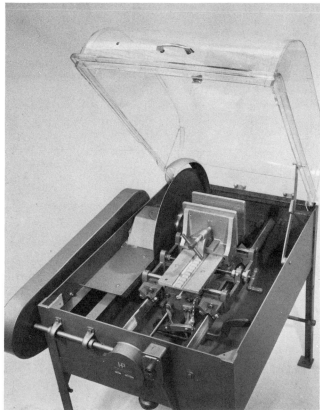

2-3.

The opposite end of the shaft from the blade holds the *pulley* over which passes a *V-belt*. This connects the shaft to the motor.

The *vise*, or *clamp*, holds the material to be cut. There are several different designs on the market: the important consideration is that it holds the rock firmly enough not to slip during cutting. Wooden clamps are best; steel clamps should be lined with wood or Masonite to give a better gripping surface.

Standard vises often cannot clamp small, irregularly shaped pieces or butt ends firmly enough to be slabbed from end to end. For this purpose there are several *auxiliary clamps* (2-4) on the market. With one of these every square inch of material in a piece can be slabbed, and special shapes can also be preformed accurately.

The *carriage* of the slab saw is mounted on a *track*, which carries it and the vise on a parallel course to the blade. The carriage may roll on the track on ball bearings or slide on sleeve bearings: both give good service. It is of the utmost importance that the track be set in perfect alignment with the blade. If it is not, the blade will tend to bind in the cut or even to jam, which can damage the blade. It can also burn out the motor if the saw is unattended and there is no automatic cutoff or slipping-clutch arrangement on the machine.

The feed mechanism may be one of several types. A *screw feed* moves the carriage by means of a long screw that passes through the carriage base and runs the full length of the track. A *hydraulic feed* (2-5) is operated by water pressure working through a hydraulic cylinder. Water pressure in the cylinder forces the piston to push the carriage along the track. Speed is regulated by an adjustable pressure valve on the waterline. A straight *weight feed* (2-6) pulls the carriage along the track by means of a cord or wire, which passes through a hole in the back of the box. It hangs down over a pulley and has an adjustable weight attached to the end. The cord can also pass over a pulley mounted on the inside of the back wall and return to the front, where it passes through a hole in the front wall and hangs down over a pulley with a weight at the end. This arrangement makes it easier to change the weights. A *swing-arm weight feed* (2-7) saw does not have a carriage that travels on a track. The rock clamp is on the end of an arm, which is fastened at the other end with a hinge attached to a bar near the top of the hood over the blade. This allows the rock in the clamp to swing down in an arc and make contact with the blade. Pressure is supplied by a weight on the end of a cord similar to the system on the regular weight-feed saw. All of these systems are efficient and produce smooth cuts,

2-4.

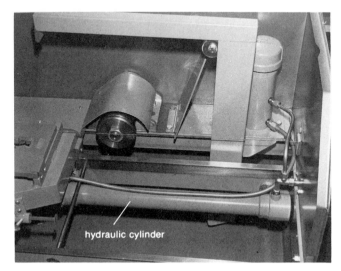

2-5.

2-6.

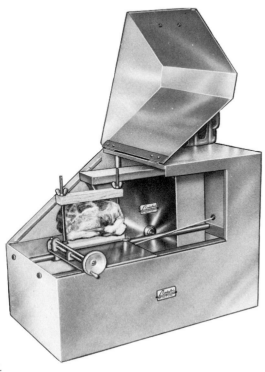

2-7.

but saws using electrical power leave very slight ridges due to the fluctuations of the alternating current. This does not occur with hydraulic and weight-feed systems because the pressure remains constant.

A slabbing saw should provide some means of adjusting the rate of feed for materials of different hardness or size. Some saws are equipped with a device that automatically adjusts the pressure to the amount of resistance that the material presents. A slipping clutch will prevent damage to the blade and motor if for some reason there is too much resistance. Some models also have an automatic cutoff switch that stops the motor when the cut is completed.

A word should be said about *mud saws*, although these are seldom used for slabbing. The ancient Chinese used them as far back as the Bronze Age. A mixture of water and abrasive grit is used as the cutting agent. The saw may be of any operational type: some sectioning saws are used with mud. The blade is bare metal without teeth of any kind. The grit clings to the relatively soft metal and abrades the stone.

Although regular slabbing saws can be used with mud, it is not practical because the grit would wear the moving parts. The swing-arm weight-feed saw operates very well with mud because it has no moving parts. Comparatively small hand-fed mud saws can be made for blades up to 12″. With a steady rest in front of the blade the operator can make sectioning cuts by holding the piece in his hands. This is both tedious and messy but practical for small pieces, and these saws are inexpensive compared with other saws. They are necessarily homemade, and the cost for parts and materials is modest (see the section on homemade equipment in this chapter).

Some slabbing saws have auxiliary tables that equip them for trimming as well as slabbing. Larger material can be slabbed than with trim saws that have a slabbing attachment. If you want a combination saw for slabbing and trimming, your selection will depend on the maximum size of your material: if it is limited to 2″ or 3″ in thickness, the trim saw with attachments should be adequate. It is less expensive and occupies less space than the slab-saw type.

Typical *trim saws* (2-8) are similar to table saws for woodworking. The material rests on the flat table and is pushed by hand against the rotating blade. Most trim saws do not provide any means of guiding the slab in a straight line, but some models have an adjustable guide rail, or fence. With this feature perfectly straight, parallel cuts can be made. Trim-saw blades vary in size from 3″ or 4″ to 8″ or 10″. Although trim saws are used primarily for trimming slabbed materials, some of the larger models can be fitted with an auxiliary vise and track with which small pieces of rough can be slabbed (2-9).

One disadvantage of almost all trim saws is the fact that the table is set above the arbor. This is necessary for making cuts that extend beyond the vertical center of the blade, but it means that you cannot make a square inside-corner cut in a slab without leaving undercuts on the bottom side. Raising the back end of the slab at the end of the cut will avoid the undercut, but it is an imprecise procedure and usually results in a ragged corner where the two cuts meet, which must be trued with a grinder.

An auxiliary table, made of wood or metal, can be set at an angle that will allow the cut to be made on the radius of the blade (2-10). It can be slipped on the saw table whenever inside cuts must be made, but it is an awkward arrangement at best. A more efficient answer to the problem is to set the table level with the center of the blade. There is only one saw with this design on the market today (2-11). It uses a 10″ blade, which allows a straight cut of about 4 1/2″. Longer cuts require turning the slab and cutting from the other side to meet the original cut. Inner-angle cuts can be made without leaving any undercuts.

The author has converted a trim saw to make continuous long cuts and also to cut neat inner-angle corners (2-12). The front part of a standard trim-saw table was sawed off and dropped down to arbor center so that cutting is level with the center of the blade. To make a longer cut, an auxiliary table is attached. This table is tight against and level with the upper part of the original table. Most simple trim saws that do not have guide fences or attachments for slabbing can be altered in this manner. It is unfortunate that no convertible trim saw of this kind is available from manufacturers: most lapidaries would appreciate the advantages offered by this design.

Lapidary *blades* (2-13) are usually diamond-charged. They are either *notched*—diamond grit is embedded in notches in the rim—or *sintered*—a solid rim of diamond grit is fused with the metal. The two types cut with

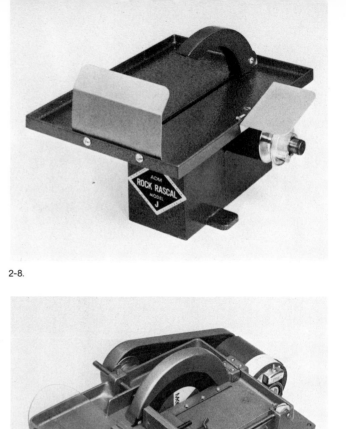

2-8.

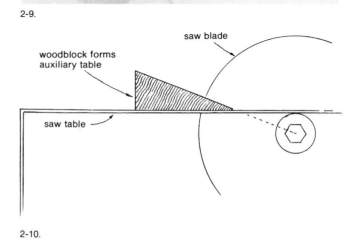

2-9.

saw blade

woodblock forms auxiliary table

saw table

2-10.

2-11.

about the same efficiency, but notched blades are more easily damaged if they are not used properly. Sintered blades cost appreciably more but last a great deal longer with normal use. A variation of the continuous sintered rim is a rim composed of segments of sintered material with short gaps between. The manufacturer claims that this design results in better cutting action, because the gaps allow more efficient flushing by the coolant. It may be reassuring to know that none of the blades will cut your finger if you touch it accidentally.

Blades for slabbing saws vary from 10" to 36" in diameter. There is a practical relationship between the diameter and the thickness of the blade: the blade must be thick enough to withstand a tendency to bend out of line under pressure. But many manufacturers offer blades of the same diameter that vary considerably in thickness, because thinner blades require less diamond than thicker ones. They wear out faster but are less expensive. The thinner blades also waste less material, an important factor with valuable and expensive stones, and they cut faster. Faceters need the thinnest practical blade for cutting materials such as ruby, sapphire, and emerald, as do cutters of fine jade, turquoise, opal, and other valuable materials that are not to be faceted. The thinnest blades must be used with great care to prevent bending under pressure. Faceting blades of very thin metal, usually copper, range from 3" to 5" in diameter. All blades must be supported by flanges of suitable width: the thinner the blade, the wider the flange in proportion to the diameter.

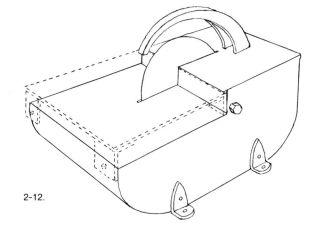

2-12.

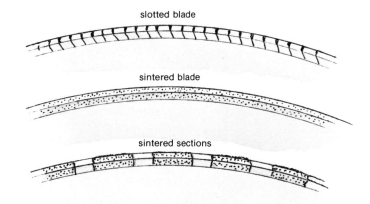

slotted blade

sintered blade

sintered sections

2-13.

Grinders

After a stone is sawed to its rough dimensions, a *grinder* is used to approximate the final shape.

A grinding machine consists of a vertical or horizontal (2-14) arbor that carries the grinding wheel or wheels, a pulley that carries the drive belt, and a splash pan and hood. It is usually driven by an electric motor. Horizontal grinders are the more popular: they allow the operator more freedom of movement and a better view. Most horizontal models can carry two or more wheels, whereas a vertical shaft can carry only one. On the other hand, a vertical shaft can be used to mount a horizontal lap plate in place of the grinding wheel, which eliminates the need for a separate flat lapping machine. A grinder should be fitted with sealed ball bearings: they require no attention and will give many years of troublefree operation. They should be protected from water and grit by a metal cup mounted on the shaft between the bearing and the flange.

Grinding is normally done on the peripheral face of the wheel. The side of the wheel can be used for light lapping. Grinding wheels must be operated with a lubricant-coolant solution, usually plain water. Its principal function is to flush away excess material, which can clog the pores of the wheel and reduce its efficiency. The water is usually supplied from a line tapped into the municipal water system. In horizontal grinders the line is connected to a regular cutoff valve located at the top of the splash guard that covers the wheel (2-15). With this setup an outlet for the water that collects in the splash pan must be provided. It should not be connected into a plumbing drain, because heavy grit from the wheel will clog the pipes. A drainpipe can be run directly outdoors, or the outlet pipe can simply drain into a large container under the bench.

Alternatives to a direct connection to the water system include filling the splash pan with water to a fraction of an inch below the bottom of the wheel. The air suction created by the speed of the wheel will pick up enough water for adequate lubrication. The only problem is to keep the water level constant: because of splash loss the supply will have to be replenished frequently. A slightly better solution is to fasten a sponge in the pan so that it touches the bottom of the wheel. A continuous supply of flowing water that can be regulated with a valve is always preferable. This can be provided without recourse to a city water system by using a small recirculating pump. The same container can be used for both the supply source and the drain outlet. The pump is placed in the tank and a plastic pipe run from it to the grinder valve. The drainpipe carries the water back into the tank, and the same water is used over and over.

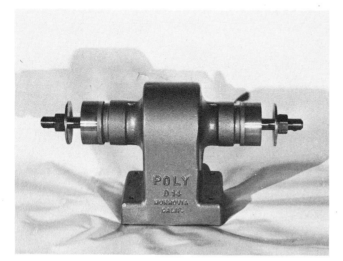

2-14.

2-15.

One problem with supplying water to vertical wheels is to spread it evenly over the face. Valves usually furnish a drip or jet to the center or to one side, leaving the rest of the wheel unlubricated. One of the best solutions is to hang a piece of heavy cloth, canvas, or lightweight carpeting from the inside of the splash hood. It should span the width of the hood and touch the wheel above the grinding area. This will distribute water over the entire face and even to some extent on the sides of the wheel and also helps to prevent spraying. It can be held in position by screwing a strip of metal to the underside of the hood (2-16).

If you don't have access to running water, you can lubricate your grinder without using a recirculating pump by simply placing a large container on a rack or shelf above the machine and running the water by gravity through a plastic or metal tube to the valve in the splash hood. The vertical-shaft grinder can be supplied with water from a valve set above the flat surface of the wheel. The water is carried across the face to the edge of the wheel by centrifugal force. It is partially absorbed by the porosity of the wheel and thrown out of the peripheral face, lubricating work done on that surface.

Lapidary *grinding wheels* are specially compounded by mixing silicon-carbide grit with a bonding agent. The mixture is molded under great pressure and heat-treated to produce a wheel that will grind hard stone efficiently. The wheels are normally 1/2″ to 2″ thick and 6″ to 12″ in diameter and are available in different grit sizes, generally from 80- to 400-mesh. Grits are graded by sifting them through screens of different sizes, and the mesh size refers to the number of screen openings per square inch: the smaller the mesh, the finer the grit, or grain, and the higher the mesh, or grain, number. Grinding wheels are supplied with various-sized arbor holes so that you can obtain a wheel of the desired specifications to fit the shaft on your particular machine.

Coarse wheels cut faster than fine wheels, but the *bond* affects the cutting rate more than the size of the grain. The bond holds the grain together, and different bonds produce different levels of hardness. The cutting action of a wheel depends on the rate at which the grains wear away as they become dull and expose fresh, sharp grains. For this reason *soft* bonded wheels cut faster than harder ones, since the dull grains wear away faster. But they also wear out faster—they become too small in diameter for practical use. If you are more interested in economy than in speed, buy the regular medium-hard bonded wheel. There is no difference in cost among wheels with different bonds.

For general work it is best to have at least two grinding wheels, a 100- or 120-grit and a 220-grit. Most lapidaries use a medium-hard bond for the fine wheel and a medium-soft bond for the coarse. A 320- or 400-grit in a medium-hard bond is useful for cutting materials that rate less than 6 in hardness. If you are limited to only one wheel, choose a coarser one: a 180-grit wheel is a good all-purpose grinder. A skillful operator can cut even very soft materials satisfactorily by using a very light touch.

As with saw blades, grinding wheels should always be used with flanges of proper diameter. They should be machined with a recess on the inner face and a flat rim at the outer edge. This rim exerts equal pressure when the nut is tightened. The diameter should be roughly one-third the diameter of the wheel.

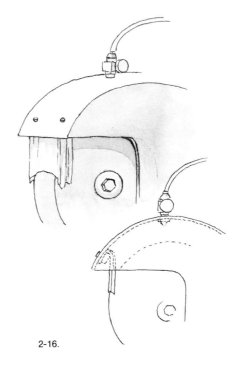

2-16.

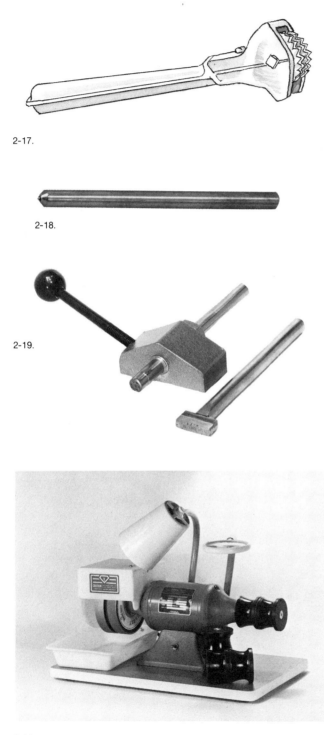

2-17.

2-18.

2-19.

2-20.

A *wheel dresser* (2-17, 2-18, and 2-19) is an important tool used to keep the grinding wheel smooth and to dress special contours on the grinding surface. It is discussed in detail in chapter 3. Instructions for making a diamond-point wheel dresser are given later in this chapter.

In recent years *diamond* grinding wheels (2-20) have become very popular for lapidary work. Flat-faced wheels for peripheral grinding; disks, both flat and cup-shaped; and flat lap wheels are available in different diameters and different grit sizes. Diamond wheels differ in structure and operation from silicon-carbide wheels. The latter depend on the erosion of dull grit to remain sharp; the former will cut as long as the grit remains in place, since diamond is harder than any other material. The grit in the surface of the wheel is bonded as permanently as possible: the more permanent the bond, the more expensive the wheel and the longer it will last. Diamond wheels are similar in use to other abrasive wheels. Heavy pressure must be avoided in grinding because the diamond particles may be torn out of the bond, shortening the life of the wheel. In spite of the relatively high initial cost diamond grinders have become popular with both amateur and professional lapidaries because they cut more rapidly and efficiently than conventional grinding wheels; they do not require dressing; they are cleaner to operate; and they last much longer.

Sanders

Sanding machines are used to smooth the stone after it has been ground to its final shape. There are three general types: *drum* (2-21), *disk* (2-22), and *belt* (2-23). The first two, like grinders, can be run either horizontally or vertically on the same arbors used for grinding wheels. Belt sanders are special machines made for sanding belts, which run on two rubber-covered pulleys.

There are also three types of sanding drums. One is essentially a metal wheel with a broad, flat rim to hold the sanding cloth. The metal rim, usually 3″ in width, is covered with either rubber, felt, or cork to act as a resilient backing for the cloth. The cloth strip, the same width as the rim, is inserted in a narrow slit in the rim and held tightly in place. An expanding drum (2-24) is a 6″ or 8″ wheel covered with a thick layer of rubber that expands with the centrifugal force exerted by the wheel. A continuous belt of sanding cloth is slipped over the wheel; it becomes tight with the speed of rotation and offers a firm but resilient sanding surface.

Disk sanders are mounted on the end of the shaft and can be used on either horizontal or vertical arbors.

There are several designs: some have a solid backing of rubber, felt, or cork; others have an open back, which allows the cloth to conform more fully to rounded contours.

Silicon-carbide cloth comes in dimensions to fit all sanders; in rolls, continuous belts, and disks; in grit sizes 120, 220, 320, 400, and 600; and in dry or wet-or-dry grades. The latter can be used with water; the former cannot.

2-23.

2-21.

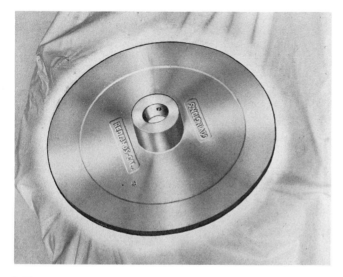

2-22.

2-24.

Rubber metal-finishing wheels are sometimes used for lapidary sanding. They can be mounted on either vertical or horizontal arbors. They are very good for sanding some of the harder materials, but due to their unyielding surface it is difficult to sand rounded contours without leaving flat spots.

Diamond sanding cloth is also available for lapidary use in strip, disk, and belt form. It can be used on standard sanding units or on machines specifically designed for it. Diamond cloth has the same advantages found in diamond grinders.

Polishers

Polishing machines are not presently manufactured as separate units: felt, wood, or leather buffs must be mounted on a homemade machine or on one of the combination or all-purpose units discussed below. The ideal polisher can be operated at slow speeds so that pressure can be applied without generating excessive heat. For best results assemble a unit with a horizontal shaft between two pillow-block bearings; this allows two wheels to be mounted vertically with a large pulley between (2-25). A motor with a small pulley will produce the slow speed required for the wheels. A splash hood, which can be closed to protect the wheels from contamination when not in use, is desirable.

Polishing *buffs* are made of different materials, depending on the stones to be polished. Solid felt wheels with various degrees of hardness, cloth buffs stitched together in layers, leather buffs of both side- and end-grain leather, and wooden wheels and laps are used with various polishing compounds for different purposes. Polishing is discussed in detail in chapter 4.

Laps

There are three kinds of *laps:* the *flat* lap, which is a flat disk that rotates horizontally on a vertical shaft; the overhead, or overarm, *oscillating* lap; and the *vibrating* lap.

The standard flat lap uses cast-iron lap plates varying from 12″ to 24″ in diameter. These plates must be carefully balanced in manufacture so that they run evenly and without vibration. The plates are threaded onto the upper end of a vertical shaft (2-26) that does not extend through the plate. This allows the entire flat surface to be used in lapping. The lower end of the shaft is set into a thrust bearing, and a ball bearing is also installed in the bench top. A large-diameter pulley is fitted on the shaft and connected to a small pulley on the motor to give the slow speed necessary to keep the grit mixture on the plate during operation. Lap plates are essentially flat with a slight crown on the surface (2-27). Perfectly flat plates would create a vacuum between the plate and the stone, which could cause it to adhere to the plate.

The overhead oscillating lap (2-28) is designed primarily for lapping large surfaces. A number of separate slabs can also be mounted level in a frame (3-16), held in place with plaster of paris, and lapped together.

2-25.

2-26.

2-27.

Vibrating laps (2-29) work automatically. The flat surface of the slab is placed on the lap, which is covered with a slurry of abrasive grit. As the lap vibrates, the pieces move over the surface and the grit mixture flattens and smooths them. Lap plates do not have to be changed but must be carefully cleaned between uses. Polishing is done on a special pad, which is placed on the lap and covered with polishing compound. Some automatic machines have an eccentric shaft attached to the plate; others have a vibrating motor underneath. In both cases the plate is set on springs, and the agitation effect is essentially the same. For designs that involve a large number of slabs automatic laps can save an enormous amount of time that would otherwise be spent on handwork.

2-29.

2-28.

All-Purpose Machines

Many amateurs and even some professionals do their work on *combination*, or *all-purpose*, *machines* that include such units as a trim saw, grinding wheels, sanding drums, and a polisher (2-30, 2-31, and 2-32). There is a wide variety of such machines on the market and they vary in size and in the number of tools. Even the largest take up a good deal less space than the corresponding separate units, and they are less expensive because they are usually operated by a single motor on a single shaft, on which the various units are mounted. On the smallest machines wheels, drums, and disks must be changed for various operations, a disadvantage from the time-saving standpoint.

2-30.

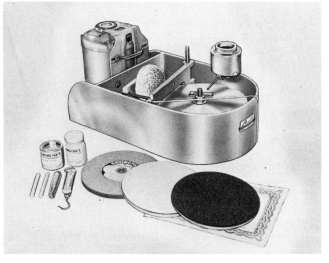

2-32.

2-31.

Bead Mills

A *bead mill* (2-33) is a comparatively simple (although fairly expensive) machine for grinding small round balls or beads automatically, not essential equipment unless you make beads in quantity. It consists of an upper and a lower plate, between which the beads are ground. The upper plate has a centered shaft, which is fastened in the chuck of a regular machinist's drill press. The lower plate, which has shallow grooves in which the beads are run, is set on springs in a tublike container that holds a grit mixture for grinding and smoothing. The bead preforms (ground roughly round by hand) are placed in the grooves on the lower plate, with the tub and plate centered under the upper plate in the drill-press chuck. The upper plate is lowered onto the beads; a slurry of silicon-carbide grit is placed in the pan to cover the lower plate; and the rotary motion of the upper plate grinds the beads perfectly round.

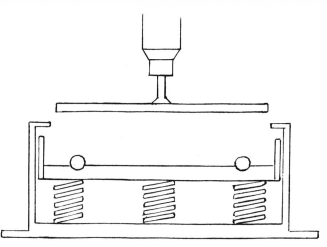

2-33.

Tumblers

A tumbler is used to grind, sand, and polish fairly small gem materials automatically. The standard machine consists of a barrel, or drum; a set of rollers, on which the drum rotates; a frame; and a pan. The simple frame for the base holds the rollers in position under the drum. One of the rollers is fitted with a pulley. A belt passes over this pulley and another pulley on an electric motor, which operates the machine. The drive roller turns the drum, which rotates on it and on the free roller. Gem materials are loaded into the drum with a slurry of silicon-carbide grit, the drum is sealed, and the motor started. As the drum turns, the material is continuously carried up the side of the drum and down again, allowing the pieces to roll against each other and be ground by the grit.

2-34.

Most tumblers are very simple and fairly inexpensive machines. The drums are made of metal, rubber, plastic, glass, wood, or combinations of these, usually lined with rubber. The shape of the drum (inside) can be either round, hexagonal, or octagonal, and it is either sealed (2-34) or open-ended. In the latter the work is visible, moreover, some materials create gas, which can build up explosive pressure in a sealed drum. A comparatively new type of machine uses a vibrating rather than a rolling action (2-35), which makes the work much faster.

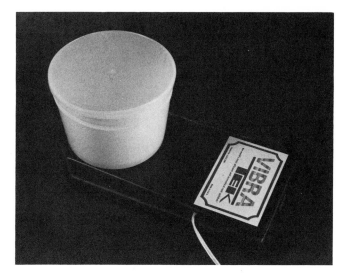

2-35.

Drilling Machines

There are a number of *drilling machines* on the market for operating the small-diameter bits used in lapidary work (2-36). In making a selection look for: an accurate *chuck*, or *collet*, to hold the drill; a sensitive control for the drill point; and a motor or speed-control system capable of at least 5,000 r.p.m. A system for changing speeds is important if you use several drills that require different speeds. Tubular drills should be operated at lower speeds than solid drills; diamond drills require higher speeds than drills used with abrasive grit. If your machine does not have a built-in speed-change system, use a *rheostat* (2-44), a simple, relatively inexpensive device that regulates speed with a foot control. Some rheostats have a bench-top control that can be set for any speed within its range.

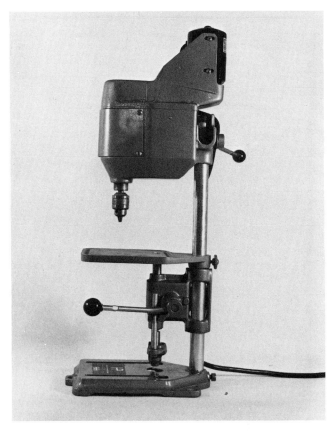

2-36.

The horsepower of the motor is not critical: it can be as low as 1/15 h.p. since very little pressure is exerted on the drill point. More important is a means of either raising the drill or lowering the pan intermittently during operation to allow water, in the case of diamond drills, or grit and lubricant, in the case of solid or tubular drills used with a slurry, to run into the hole. Hand manipulation is the most practical method for shallow holes in materials less than 7 in hardness, which require only a few minutes of drilling time. For harder materials and deeper holes an automatic lifting or lowering device is a great timesaver.

Hand-fed drills should be very sensitive to the touch, especially with small solid-diamond drill bits (less than 1 1/2mm), which are easily broken or damaged by too much pressure. This also applies to handmade diamond-chip drills. A knob control is preferable to a lever because it can be operated with the fingertips, allowing the amount of pressure to be more easily felt and controlled (3-17).

Drill presses made for wood- and metalwork are too heavy and insensitive for small lapidary drill bits, but they are generally used to operate the larger core drills (1/4" or more in diameter). Standard portable hand drills can also be used with the larger core drills if supported in drill stands made for this purpose.

A new type of drilling machine operates with ultrasonic high-frequency vibrations and is extremely efficient with any kind of gem material. It uses silicon-carbide grit and a steel-wire drill bit. Although the cost of the standard industrial machine is prohibitive for most individual craftsmen, a small model is now available at a price that many lapidaries can afford. According to the manufacturer it performs as well as the larger machine for all forms of drilling and even for carving. Laser-beam equipment is also being used for commercial drilling, but it is expensive.

Several types of drill *bits* may be used effectively with the drilling machines discussed above. The most expensive are solid, fused diamond-abrasive drills, available in sizes from 1mm to 5mm. The solid-diamond section of the bit is about 3/16" to 1/4" deep, depending on the diameter (2-37). Diamond-plated bits cost less but have a shorter life. Plated drills as small as .02" in diameter are available, but they wear out very fast, especially on hard materials. It is more economical to use small needles and diamond grit for tiny holes.

Regular steel twist drills can be used for soft materials such as some turquoise, malachite, and other stones under 5 1/2 in hardness. Most stones between 6 and 7 in hardness can be drilled satisfactorily with tungsten-carbide drills. Steel drills lose their cutting edge rather quickly because all stone material is somewhat abrasive.

Tungsten carbide loses its edge only through chipping. A drill consisting of one or two diamond chips embedded in the end of a short section of drill rod can be handmade and is very efficient. It is discussed at the end of this chapter. Drills handmade of metal tubing are very efficient for holes down to 1/32″ in diameter. They are used with a mixture of abrasive grit and water or lightweight oil. Buy hard-drawn tubing in various diameters and cut it to the required length. Gold-filled, steel, or brass tubing can be used, but not stainless steel or sterling silver. The metal should be hard enough to remain rigid in use but soft enough that the grit can embed itself in the cutting end. Steel *needle tubes* are fine for drilling with abrasive. They are supplied in eight sizes from 1/32″ to 7/64″ o.d. (see appendix 3). Brass tubing in smaller sizes is hard to find, but you can use a draw plate to draw 1/8″ tubing (a common size) down to any lesser diameter. Gold-filled tubing, which is excellent for drilling, can be obtained from jewelry-materials-supply houses in a variety of sizes.

Core drills are hollow drills that produce a usable core. Large core drills are used by geologists and mining engineers to extract earth and mineral samples; lapidaries use smaller core drills to cut out preforms for round stones and to produce the inner and outer diameters of rings and bracelets. Carvers of gem materials use them to drill apertures in carvings and to cut out the voids in hollow vessels. The minimum outside diameter is 3/32″. Small, hollow drills are usually referred to as *tube* drills when the hole rather than the core is the object of the drilling.

Diamond-impregnated core drills (2-38) for lapidary use and other industrial applications have a shank that is fitted into the chuck of a drill press for operation. The shank can be a fixed part of the drill or a separate piece screwed into the head. These drills come in a wide range of sizes: 1/64″ increments from 3/32″ to 5″ and more in diameter are available. Plain steel core drills (2-39) are used with a slurry of abrasive grit. They are much slower than the diamond drills. They are available in increments up to 40mm i.d. and o.d. and in standard ring half-sizes from 4 to 14 1/2.

2-38.

2-39.

2-37.

Carving Machines

Lapidary carving usually involves work measuring not more than 1' or so in any dimension. Larger sculpture is beyond the scope of this book. There are two basic types of *carving machines: stationary* and *hand-held.* In the former the machine remains fixed, and the work is manipulated against a rotating cutting wheel or point. In the latter the machine itself is held in the hand and applied to the work. The author prefers the stationary type because it allows greater control. A stationary horizontal arbor (2-40) was used by ancient Chinese carvers and is still universally used in China today. It is also the preferred tool in gem engraving and cameo carving, which require maximum control. Hand-held machines either have a flexible shaft powered by a stationary motor (2-41) or a self-contained motor (2-42). The former type is much smaller than the bulkier motor-contained tool and easier to control.

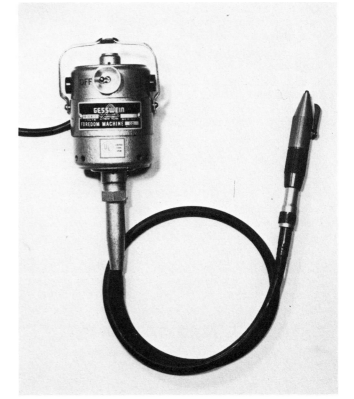

2-41.

2-40.

2-42.

Stationary arbors are quite variable in design: some have self-contained motors; others are operated by belts and pulleys from an auxiliary motor. The essential features of a good carving machine are a chuck, or collet, that runs true; smooth operation; a motor that does not overheat; and a mounting that allows adequate working space around the cutting point. If you use diamond tools, high speed is important. They cut slowly at speeds under 10,000 r.p.m., and, if you apply pressure to speed them up, the diamond particles can be torn out of the bond. A plated tool can be ruined completely in just a few minutes.

Diamond and bonded-silicon-carbide tools require a supply of water to prevent excessive heating of the material and the tool, to flush away excess material, and to allow a clear view of the work. The problems of water supply and splash seem to baffle many carvers. Some mount their machine with the axis pointing straight at the operator—any splash is thrown sideward, not in the carver's face. But better visibility and control are possible if the edge of the cutting tool is lined up with the eye— that is, with the arbor parallel to the front of the bench. Chinese carvers solved the problem of splash by bending a wide strip of bamboo to form a shield over the tool. By looking just past the edge of the strip the carver's eye was in almost perfect alignment with edge of the tool, yet the bamboo strip caught any splash of the grit. They did not need a water drip. The author's solution to the problem of water supply is to install a valve in the top of a metal strip bent over the tool, which acts as a splash guard (2-43). A short length of tubing extends from the valve to a convenient height above the work. The other end is inserted in a container of water mounted above the bench, forming a syphon that is controlled by regulating the valve.

Some lapidary carving machines can be adjusted to a vertical position and used as a drill. Most have small motors that run a maximum of 5,000 r.p.m., an adequate speed except for diamond tools. Some drills (2-36) can be turned horizontally and used as a carving machine. Many readily available motors can be adapted for carving, particularly with wet abrasives. They can also be used with silicon-carbide wheels and points if high speed is not a requirement. For carving with silicon-carbide grits and soft iron tools a low speed is necessary to avoid throwing the grit off the tool and the work. Even a portable hand drill, mounted in a suitable horizontal stand installed on the bench, makes an acceptable inexpensive carving machine. It must be controlled by a rheostat (2-44) to obtain the low speed required.

2-43.

2-44.

33

Engraving machines are in principle similar to carving machines. They require a high degree of accuracy and freedom from any kind of vibration. Most gem engravers prefer a small lathe such as that used by jewelers and watchmakers because of its precision. The collets of such lathes assure absolute concentricity of the rotation. All but very small-scale engraving can be done on the high-precision carving machines discussed above.

The wheels, saws, and points used in carving can be made of *diamond* (2-45) *silicon-carbide* (2-46) or soft *metal* (used with wet abrasive grit). The first two types are available from dealers; the last must be handmade. Diamond tools can be *plated*—diamond grit is deposited in a metal coating on the surface; *solid-impregnated*, or *sintered*, which contain diamond grit throughout; or *embedded* with grit in notches and nicks in the surface, which must be handmade. Well-made diamond-plated tools will serve efficiently when operated with due care; impregnated or sintered tools are much more durable. Homemade tools are adequate for most work and can be recharged with grit when necessary. They can be made for only a fraction of the cost of manufactured diamond tools. Instructions are provided later in this chapter.

There are many sizes and shapes of silicon-carbide points and wheels on the market that can be used for carving. They are permanently mounted on shanks varying from 3/32″ to 1/4″ in diameter. The only difficulty is in obtaining tools with the proper bond for lapidary work: the standard bond is designed for grinding metals and is too hard for all but the softest stones. Silicon-carbide tools should be ordered from the manufacturer with the required bond specified.

Steel tools (2-47) can be used to carve and shape materials less than 5 in hardness. Burrs, points, and wheels designed for soft metals, woodworking, and dentistry can be used. Rotary steel tools (4-38) are useful for roughing out carvings in softer materials. Rubber abrasive wheels for sanding and semipolishing (2-48) can be used effectively on some materials, although they are primarily designed for metal. They are made in a variety of shapes and sizes and in a number of grits from coarse to superfine. Very thin silicon-carbide separating disks, are extremely useful for carving.

2-45.

2-46.

2-47.

All the unmounted wheels mentioned above are mounted on standard small arbors, or mandrels, which come in diameters of 3/32″ and 1/8″ and are 1 1/2″ long. The wheels are mounted with a screw. Similar arbors are made to mount small rubber-covered sanding drums (2-49), which are very handy for small carvings, particularly in tight recesses. Sanding sleeves are slipped over the drum and tightened in place by screwing in the mandrel, which causes the drum to expand. The drums are made in diameters of 1/4″, 1/2″ and 3/4″. A similar 2″ rubber-covered drum (2-49) is used by woodworkers for sanding curves. It has aluminum-oxide sanding sleeves and works effectively on ivory and other relatively soft materials under 6 in hardness. All of these miniature and small sanding sleeves can be recharged with fresh silicon-carbide grit or recovered with fresh silicon-carbide cloth. (The aluminum-oxide sleeves will not work on harder materials.) The cloth must be cut to fit exactly with a diagonal joint. The sleeve is mounted on the mandrel and coated with an adhesive, and the cloth is attached and held in place with a rubber band until the adhesive has set.

2-49.

2-48.

Faceting Machines

A simple *faceting machine* consists of a *dop stick*, one end of which holds the stone; a *backrest*, which supports the other end of the stick; a rotating circular metal *lap plate*, on which the stone rests; and a source of power to turn the lap plate.

The oldest and simplest faceting setup is the *jamb peg* (2-50). It is essentially a dop stick of metal or wood, one end of which fits into any of a number of shallow holes, or sockets, in a backrest located alongside the lap plate. The backrest may be either a small, flat panel of wood or metal mounted on a rigid post or an inverted rotating cone on a vertical center shaft, in which holes are spaced around the cone in rows at different levels. To operate the jamb peg, the sharpened end of the stick is fitted into the hole that provides the desired angle to the stone resting on the lap plate. The stone is held in place on the lap, which is covered with abrasive, until a facet is cut. In standard practice the stick is rotated in consecutive steps until the entire stone has been faceted. The stick is moved from hole to hole to set the angles necessary for the different rows of facets. In older machines the lap plate was connected to a gear and a handle, which the operator turned with one hand while holding the dop stick with the other. Modern machines use an electric motor for power.

Nearly all amateurs and most professionals today use a faceting machine that provides calibrated settings for both the vertical and rotary angles of the facets (2-51).

These angles are prescribed in diagrams that are available for all the standard cuts now in use, which eliminates the need for skill on the part of the operator in setting the angles. The only skill still required lies in cutting the facets to the proper depth so that the stone is geometrically perfect when finished and in attaining a perfect polish. The rotary-

2-51.

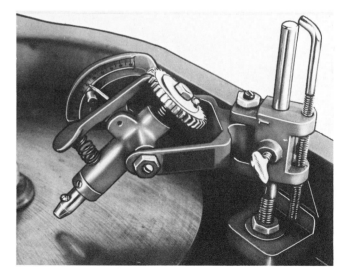

2-52.

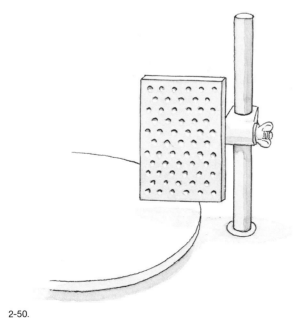

2-50.

36

lap arbor is provided with a round base plate on which are mounted lap plates, or wheels, of different materials, such as copper, iron, lead, tin, nylon, and bakelite. These are charged with various grinding and polishing compounds for different materials.

Since a number of different lap plates are required in order to work a variety of faceting materials, a complete setup can be quite costly. There is an inexpensive faceting head on the market designed to be used on a small, multipurpose lapidary machine (2-52). Although complex cuts can be difficult to achieve with this machine, it is certainly adequate for experimental work. It can be adapted to fit the master lap assemblies used with more expensive faceting heads. Another inexpensive option is a homemade jamb-peg assembly: a good mechanic should be able to make one with no trouble.

Homemade Equipment
As mentioned at the beginning of this chapter, many lapidaries find it desirable to build most, if not all, of their equipment. Individuals with mechanical ability and ingenuity, along with good machine tools, can save a great deal of money in setting up a lapidary shop. Others with less skill, equipment, and experience can still find it advantageous to buy parts for the various units and assemble them into complete machines. Some manufacturers supply basic parts in kit form with instructions on how to assemble them and build the other necessary parts that are not provided. Anyone with ordinary skill can take advantage of the savings offered by these kits. Instructions and suggestions are given here for building or assembling a number of items that may be practical for particular situations. This section is by no means exhaustive: many other valuable ideas can be found in lapidary magazines and books (see the bibliography).

Saws
Slabbing saws and trim saws are usually assembled from parts provided by various manufacturers. Some are in kit form, and it is necessary to construct only the tank, the box that holds the assembly, and the hood that covers it. A slabbing saw can be built from scratch (2-53) without parts specifically manufactured for the purpose, except for the arbor (2-54), pulleys, and belt. The stone is fed into the saw by a weight-feed arrangement. Cross-feed is accomplished by sliding the arm assembly on the overhead rod and hand setting the thickness to be cut. This saw does not have the precision of a manufactured machine, but it will do very acceptable slabbing. A simple trim saw (2-55) can also be easily constructed with a manufactured arbor (2-56).

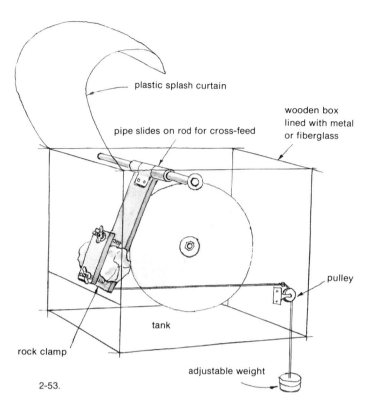

2-53.

2-54.

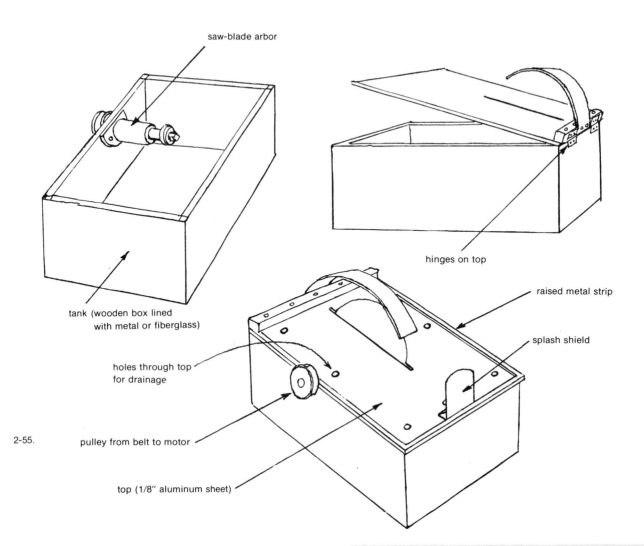

saw-blade arbor

hinges on top

tank (wooden box lined
with metal or fiberglass)

raised metal strip

splash shield

holes through top
for drainage

2-55.

pulley from belt to motor

top (1/8″ aluminum sheet)

2-56.

38

Grinders

Making a grinding machine of the standard type, which carries two grinding wheels in tandem on a horizontal shaft, is a job for a machinist. A person with average skill and tools can make the splash pans and hoods (2-57) that complete a grinding setup with galvanized sheet metal. It is rather difficult to bend the metal without a metal brake, but you can cut out the parts and have a tin shop bend them at nominal cost. The two splash pans for the standard two-wheel arbor are assembled by soldering the joints with soft solder.

A basic arbor (2-58) can be used to set up a multi-purpose machine. It has a shaft to support either two or four wheels in tandem, plus mounting space at the ends for flat disks or other attachments. The beginner can start with one or two wheels and add others gradually to make up a unit of grinders, sanders, and polisher. The savings are not significant, but the expense is spread out conveniently.

A single-wheel grinder is much less expensive and much easier to make. Different sizes of single-end arbors with sealed bearings are available from lapidary manufacturers (2-59). With one of these and a 1/4-horsepower motor it is simple to set up a grinding unit for one wheel, which can also be used for a sanding drum or disk and even for a polishing wheel if you avoid contaminating it with grit from the grinding and sanding operations.

2-58.

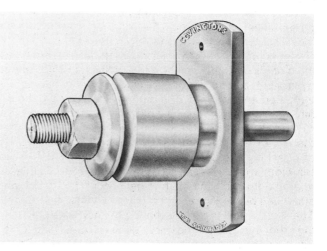

2-59.

2-57.

Sanders

Any of the units just discussed can be used to mount sanding drums. It is impractical to make a sanding drum to mount the regular sanding-cloth strips, since the manufactured drums are made of cast aluminum, which is light and strong, equipped with a locking device that holds the cloth tight, and inexpensive. Disk sanders are not expensive either, but a satisfactory substitute (2-60) can be easily made with a circular piece of wood plank with a hole bored in the center to fit the arbor shaft. The area around the hole is recessed so that a nut can be screwed on the arbor below the surface of the disk. It will not interfere with the sanding cloth, and the whole surface can be used. Select an even-grained plank of well-seasoned wood at least 3/4″ thick. The tendency of the wood to warp can be minimized by applying two or three coats of shellac. Three types can be made: flat, slightly convex, or with a concave recess. The flat type is covered with 1/4″-thick sponge-rubber sheet; the convex type, with thin sheet cork; the recessed type, with the sanding cloth alone, which is stretched tightly over the hollow recess. In all three types the cloth is brought over the edge and held in place either by cement, a snap rim of flat metal, or a wire that can be tightened and secured. The perimeter of the disk should have a shallow groove to hold the band in place. The cloth disk must be notched around the edge to fit over the rim of the disk without wrinkling. A simple method of attaching the sanding cloth to the sander is to coat the cloth with Peel-Em-Off cement, press it into place, and smooth out. The cloth is held securely in position, and it can be peeled off and replaced when it is worn out. The wooden disks can be shaped by mounting them on the arbor and contouring with regular wood-turning tools. Sanding can also be done on wooden wheels using loose abrasive grains mixed with water (see chapter 9). The wheel should not be shellacked but treated with linseed oil, which penetrates the grain and helps to prevent the absorption of moisture.

Although it is not very practical to make sanding cloth from scratch, it is quite simple to recoat a manufactured cloth when the original surface wears out. Mix a glue solution of medium (spreadable) consistency and coat the individual strips or disks, evenly. Waterproof or ordinary glue can be used, depending on whether you do wet or dry sanding. Lay the strips and disks out on newspapers and cover the coated surfaces completely with grit. A perforated flour sifter can be used to spread the grit. Pick up the covered strips by the ends, turn them over, shake off the excess grit, and spread them out, grit side up, to dry.

Polishers

A polishing unit is fairly simple to make, as described earlier in this chapter (2-25). Felt, cloth, and leather buffing wheels can also be made at home. Hard-felt buffs require special industrial equipment, but softer wheels can be made by cutting out disks of various fabrics and stitching them together to the suitable thickness on a heavy sewing machine. Fabric materials can be cemented with waterproof glue. Leave at least a 1″ unfastened margin around the outer edges. A center hole can be punched with a hole cutter made of sharpened pipe or tubing. Experiment with different fabrics: some carpeting makes an excellent buff for polishing quartz-family minerals and other stones. Cut it into a strip and apply it to the edge of a 2″-thick wooden wheel or cut it into a disk for the flat face. Soft felt 1/4″ to 1/2″ thick can also be applied to the flat surface of any disk. Canvas is another very practical material; waterproof glue should be used.

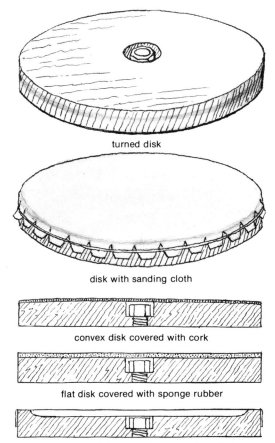

turned disk

disk with sanding cloth

convex disk covered with cork

flat disk covered with sponge rubber

2-60.

concave disk covered with sanding cloth

Wooden wheels can be covered with leather, which gives excellent results with almost every kind of material. Thin leather can be stretched over a concave disk for a resilient polishing surface or over a convex or flat disk for a hard surface. End-grain leather sometimes works better than side-grain for certain materials; to obtain an end-grain surface, a number of leather disks must be cemented together to make a thick wheel with a wide polishing surface. It can then be used for both end-grain and side-grain polishing. Bare wooden wheels are excellent for polishing hard materials such as ruby with diamond paste. The edge face is used, often with grooves turned in the surface to accommodate different sizes and shapes of stones. Wooden wheels can be made with regular wood-turning tools.

Carving Machines and Carving Tools

Several kinds of *carving machines* can be made from readily available parts and motors. Any ball-bearing arbor that can be fitted with a multiple-step pulley on one end and a chuck on the other can be used for carving, and almost any fractional horsepower motor can be used by mounting a chuck directly on the shaft. The driving speed cannot be changed on this machine; some carvers set up two or three motors to obtain different speeds. The smaller brush-type motors can be used with a rheostat to change speeds.

Many of the rotary points and wheels for carving are homemade—some by necessity, since there are no commercial equivalents. This is particularly true of the soft metal tools used with loose abrasives and water or oil (2-61). These can be made from annealed (softened) tool-steel 1/8" and 1/4" round drill-rod stock. The end of the rod must be fully annealed by heating it to a cherry-red color and cooling it slowly by covering with borax or powdered asbestos. The blank tool is then chucked into the carving machine, and the softened end is turned to the desired contour with a sharp file as it rotates. This can be done quite accurately by using different-shaped needle files or heavier round, square, or triangular files. A jeweler's or model maker's lathe can also be used to form the heads mechanically. The work is more accurate but much slower, and precision is not essential for these tools. It is not really necessary to use tool-steel stock: nails and bolts can be cut to the proper length and turned with files just as easily. They are not uniformly straight to begin with, but the turning process trues them perfectly. Make the tool blank longer than required and true the whole shank with the file. You can then cut off the end in the chuck and reinsert the trued-up end before shaping the head. The heads of nails and bolts are larger

in diameter than the shanks and can be turned into larger shapes for slitting, incising, and grinding larger cuts.

Satisfactory diamond-charged tools can also be made by the craftsman. Saw blades from 1/2" to 3" in diameter can be slotted and charged with diamond grit by following this procedure. Cut out a disk from rolled steel, nickel silver, copper, or brass sheet with a jeweler's saw. Drill a center hole to fit the arbor. Mount the disk on the machine and true the contour with a piece of silicon-carbide grinding wheel or dressing block while it is running. Use a steady rest and make the blank perfectly true. Remove it from the arbor and place it in a vise. Disks from 2" to 3" in diameter should be placed between pieces of Masonite or other thin board, leaving only a small segment exposed. With a sharp knife or hacksaw blade make notches in the disk by striking the back of the blade against the edge at a 30° angle with a light riveting hammer. The notches should be as uniform in depth as possible and about 1/8" apart (somewhat less for smaller blades). Nick the exposed section, then turn the disk to expose more area, moving around the edge. Make a paste of diamond grit—a mixture of 50-mesh and 100-mesh—and enough Vaseline to make it workable. Put the blade back in the vise, fill the exposed notches with grit, using a splinter, and tap them shut with a light hammer. Turn the blade and proceed until all the notches are closed and tapped shut. Carefully clean off the excess mixture with the splinter and place it in a small container for future use—diamond grit is fairly expensive.

2-61.

These blades can be made with any gauge of metal. Thinner blades cut faster but need to be recharged sooner. Smaller blades from 1" to 1/2" can be made in thicknesses up to 1/8"; thicker blades resemble grinders and are very useful in carving. These smaller blades can be charged by installing them on small mandrels and closed by holding them on a plate (a slab of jade is good) in a smear of the diamond mixture and tapping the notches shut while turning the mandrel (2-62). The diamond mixture helps to fill up any uneven notches.

Carving points can also be charged with diamond grit by nicking the surface with a blade, applying the grit mixture, closing the nicks, and embedding the grit by tapping on the block or plate with a light hammer. These tools should be made of copper or brass rather than iron because the former is softer, can be more easily nicked, and holds the grit better. Soft brass is even better than copper for the finest grit (600- to 1200-mesh) and results in a very smooth finish. After nicking the tool, roll it in the diamond mixture on the plate. Use heavy pressure to embed the grit in both the nicks and the in-between surface.

Copper carving tools can also be made by melting bits of copper held on the ends of steel-drill-rod shanks into balls. The steel should be filed with deep notches to hold the ball in place; the copper will not fuse to the steel. The balls will not be symmetrical but can be trued with a file while turning in the chuck. Various shapes can be turned from the irregular masses. Pits and holes will be left in the copper, but they help to hold the diamond grit. Cylindrical shapes can be made by wrapping copper wire around the mandrel end and soldering in place. The coils are flattened by tapping, trued with a file, and charged as described above (2-63).

Very small tools for fine engraving are always made with soft copper points, since this material holds the grit better than other metals. These tiny points are too small to be nicked and must be charged by running them fairly slowly and touching them to an agate slab smeared with a mixture of 600-mesh diamond grit and oil. Some engravers insist on using olive oil, but lightweight machine oil is just as good. The grit charges the tool by embedding itself in the surface of the metal.

Wooden tools with the same shapes as the carving tools are used to polish the cuts with fine diamond paste. Because of its even grain and hardness boxwood is the preferred material. It is sold in sticks and blocks by jewelers-supply houses. Even-grained maple, apple, pear, and holly can also be used. Larger wooden tools can be used to polish the recesses in small carvings.

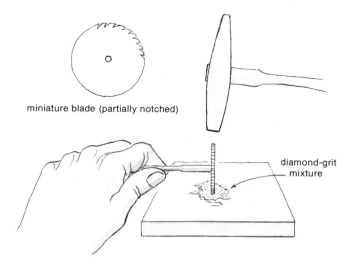

miniature blade (partially notched)

diamond-grit mixture

2-62.

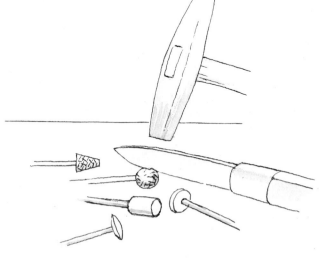

2-63.

Small Grinding Tools

There are no small grinding wheels (1 1/2″ to 3″ in diameter × 1/4″ to 1/2″ thick) suitable for lapidary use on the market. Wheels for grinding metals have such hard bonds that they will grind only the softest stone. These small, inexpensive wheels on 1/4″ mandrels are available from most hardware stores; they are worth buying just for the mandrels (not sold separately), which can be used to mount homemade wheels.

One method for making small grinding wheels is to cut down worn-out regular wheels to the desired dimensions. Wheels 1/4″ thick can be cut on a trim saw and roughly rounded up on a grinder. Too much trimming should not be done on the saw; it wears away a good deal of the metal that holds the diamond grit. The 1/4″ and 1/2″ wheels can be broken into usable sizes with a hammer. Score them for breaking by chipping out lines for the breaks. Wheels that are too thick to be useful as small grinders can be sliced in two edgewise with the slabbing saw. Drill holes to fit the wheel on the arbor with a broken section of a triangular steel file fitted into a drill press. The wheel should be thoroughly soaked in water to lubricate the drill. Mount the wheels on the arbors and put in the chuck of the carving machine. Run the machine at a fairly slow speed to start and with a wheel dresser (the single-diamond type is best) dress the wheel until it is perfectly true. Special contours can be turned on the face of the wheel as desired.

Another method of making small grinding wheels is even easier. You can make wheels of any dimensions and vary the bond to suit your needs, but you do need a ceramic kiln, enameling kiln, or wax burnout furnace with a pyrometer. Combine equal amounts of loose silicon-carbide grit (any size) and white ceramic clay. Mix thoroughly with water to the consistency of bread dough. Roll out with a rolling pin to the thickness desired for the wheels: 1/8″ to 1/2″ is the most useful thickness. Cut out the wheels with circular cookie cutters or make cutters from tubular material of appropriate diameter—from 1″ to 3″. Small tin cans can be used for the larger wheels: solder a tube in the exact center of the bottom section, extending the full depth of the cutter, and run it through, leaving a small amount of the tube on the upper side. Make sure that it is perpendicular to the bottom of the can. This enables the center hole to be cut at the same time as the wheel. If you use an open-ended can, solder on a crosspiece to hold the center tube (2-64). The center tube should be the diameter of the arbor on which the finished wheel is mounted. Let the wheels dry until they are firm enough to handle but still moist, then turn them over to keep them from warping. When they reach the stage that potters call "leather-hard," fit them on the mandrels, then remove and lay them out flat again. Let the wheels dry for at least 2 days and fire them for 1 hour or longer at 1,860° Fahrenheit. Put them on their mandrels and run them in the machine while truing them and shaping the contours with a diamond-point wheel dresser. The bond hardness and strength of the wheels can be varied by using more or less of the ceramic glaze; the more glaze, the harder and slower-cutting the wheel. Start with the 50% mixture and vary the amount of glaze slightly, both more or less, until you find the best mixture for your purpose.

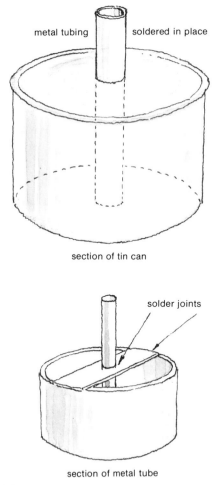

metal tubing   soldered in place

section of tin can

solder joints

section of metal tube

2-64.

The speed at which the wheels should be run will vary, depending on the diameter. An abrasive wheel works better at higher speeds: at slow speeds it will wear excessively. Experiment to find the right speed. Use heavier arbors as the size of the wheels increases: do not use mandrels less than 1/8" in diameter even for small ceramic wheels. Use 1/4" arbors on all wheels from 1 1/2" to 3", regardless of thickness.

You can make grinding points such as balls and cylinders with the same material by forming the shapes by hand on ends of drill-rod sections. Be sure to file notches at the end of the rods on which they are formed to keep the points from loosening and turning. After firing true them with a wheel dresser. You can also make useful hand tools by shaping the material into small rods with different cross-sectional shapes (2-65), somewhat like the stone slips used to sharpen woodcarving gouges and chisels. These are very convenient for working into openings and other areas in carvings that are difficult to reach with rotary tools. The work is lubricated with water, and the tool is pushed back and forth with a filing action.

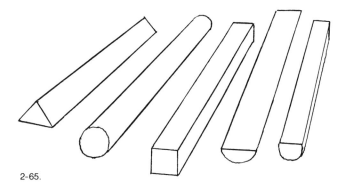

2-65.

Shellac Sanding Tools

Shellac sanding tools were used with great success by Chinese carvers for prepolishing jade. To make the tools, dry 400-mesh silicon-carbide grain and flake shellac are mixed together thoroughly in a 2-to-1 ratio, heated in a pan until the shellac dissolves, and stirred and mixed until it is a homogeneous mass. Pour the mixture onto a flat surface of stone, glass, or metal and fold it over several times with a spatula. It is then rolled out into a sheet the thickness of the desired wheels, and the wheels are cut out in whatever diameters you want. Center holes are easily made by piercing the wheels with a hot iron rod of proper diameter and truing with a cylindrical grinding point. Point tools can be made by dipping shanks into the shellac mixture while it is quite hot and picking up a small mass on the end. After it cools sufficiently, it can be molded with the fingers to the approximate shape and trued up accurately in the chuck of a carving machine, using a silicon-carbide stick or a fragment of a broken grinding wheel. The wheels are mounted on their arbors and trued up in the same manner.

Drilling Tools

Drilling machines are rather complicated to build because some mechanism must be incorporated to feed the work to the drill. Either the pan holding the work must be lowered away from the bit or the drill must be raised from the work at frequent intervals to allow the water to lubricate the hole or, with grit and water, to allow the slurry to run into the hole. Some hand-held motor tools can be mounted on the post of a small, sensitive drill press and used for drilling. These machines run at speeds that are practical for diamond drill bits (at least 5,000 r.p.m.).

Another possibility is to mount a standard portable hand drill in one of the presses made for this purpose. The maximum speed of such drills is too slow for diamond-bit drilling, but they are adequate for abrasive grit. Either solid-metal bits, small metal tubes, or large core drills can be used with this setup.

As mentioned earlier in this chapter, there is one kind of diamond drill bit that must be homemade. The special drill referred to here has a point made of either one or two diamond chips set in the end of a rod that forms the shank. These chips should be made of *carbonado*, or black-diamond crystals, which are slightly harder and tougher than other diamonds and do not chip or fracture easily. Select the fragments carefully. A section of drill rod should be used for the shank. For drills of 2mm diameter a 3/32" rod can be used. The end that holds the diamond is turned down in a tapered section to avoid binding in the hole. The end is slotted with a jeweler's saw to hold the chip. The diamond is forced into the slot, and the metal is pinched over and around it with needle-nosed pliers. Anneal the very end of the rod so that the metal can be pinched over easily. Pinch very carefully to avoid splitting or chipping the diamond. Place bits of silver solder in any gaps in the metal and melt them with the torch to make a firm seat for the chip. Dip the tip in water while it is still hot to harden and strengthen the metal. Examine the tip with a magnifier and file away any projections that will interfere with clearance (2-66). Larger drills can be made with two chips set side by side.

They will drill faster than a single-point drill. These drills are difficult to make, particularly in smaller sizes, but the results are well worth the effort. Well-made drills bore small holes through hard materials faster than most other types of drills.

Two types of core drills can be made by hand: the bare metal type that is used with a slurry of silicon-carbide grit and the slotted type that is charged with diamond grit. A machinist's skill and equipment are highly desirable since the drills must be made with precision in order to run accurately and without wobbling. To make these drills, you need a drill press and hard-soldering equipment. The tubing for the drill must be cut at a perfect right angle to the vertical axis.

To make a core drill for silicon-carbide grit, cut out a metal disk from sheet metal at least 1/8″ thick and the same diameter as the inside diameter of the tube with a jeweler's saw. Fit this piece inside the drill tube at one end and hard-solder it in place. It must be perfectly flush with the squared end of the tube. Find the exact center of the head plate and centerpunch it. Fasten the drill tube to the base plate of the drill press. If the tube has a perfectly squared end, it will be exactly perpendicular to the base plate. It can be cemented in place with dop wax or paraffin and at the same time centered under the point of the drill in the chuck of the press. The wax ensures that the tube will not move during drilling. With a sharp twist drill the exact diameter of the rod for the shank, drill a hole through the head plate. Remove the drill from the chuck and insert the shank rod. Press the shank into the hole in the plate by lowering the chuck with the handle of the drill press. Push it through the plate and let it project slightly on the underside. Hard-solder the shank in place with the chuck holding it in a perfectly centered and vertical position. To finish the drill, saw three or four vertical slots in the wall of the tube at the cutting end to allow the sludge to circulate freely in the cut underneath the drill. Drills of all sizes can be made by this method.

You can charge the drills with diamond grit by following the procedure described above for small circular saws. The end of the tube is nicked with a knife blade; the nicks are filled with the diamond grit-vaseline mixture; and the slots are closed by tapping lightly with a small hammer. You can also buy bare-metal core drills and charge them with diamond grit in the same way.

A more economical means of making core drills is to buy a carpenter's hole saw. This is a head equipped with a nest of tubular saws in diameters ranging from 1″ to 2 1/2″ in 1/4″ increments (2-67). The saws are removed and the solid center drill sawed off, and solid metal tubes in the same diameters as the original saws are substituted. These need only be drilled through the side to accept the screws that held the original saws in place. Each saw, or tube, has its own seat, and any one of the tubes can be used separately in the base, or head. They can be used for drilling with abrasive slurry or charged with diamond grit. The original hole-saw set is quite inexpensive.

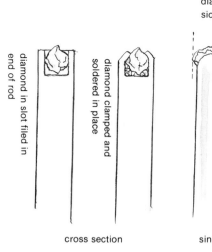
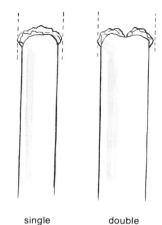

diamond projects beyond sides of shank for clearance

diamond in slot filed in end of rod

diamond clamped and soldered in place

cross section   single   double

2-66.

2-67.

Wheel Dressers

Perhaps the most useful type of wheel dresser is the single-diamond point. With it the face of a wheel can be shaped to any desired contour. It can be homemade with a soldering torch at a saving of several dollars.

There are two ways to make the dresser. Diamond crystals of various sizes are sold mounted in the ends of sections of round steel rods 1″ or so long and cost less than half as much as the regular diamond-point dressers of similar size. To finish the dresser, solder the rod into a brass or copper tube that fits and cut the tube off to the proper length.

A still less expensive procedure is to buy a loose crystal and mount it in the end of a steel rod. The crystal should be the carbonado variety, an industrial grade of diamond that is tougher than gem grades. Buy a crystal weighing 1/4 to 1/2 carat. To make the seat, drill a shallow hole just large enough to accommodate the diamond in the end of the rod and hold it slightly below the surface. With a chasing tool or a metal punch drive the metal over the diamond in as many places as possible. To assure a tight fit, before driving the metal over place small snippets of silver solder in all the gaps surrounding the diamond. After it is secured in place by tapping, heat with a torch until the solder melts and fills any gaps that are left. To finish, grind away the metal to expose just the point of the crystal (2-68).

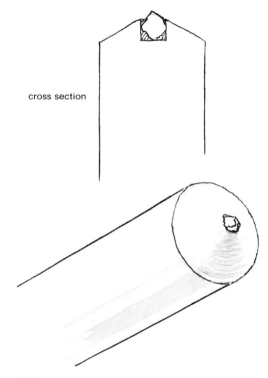

cross section

2-68.

3. Basic Techniques

The creative lapidary employs tools, materials, and techniques as a means of expressing his unique artistic ideas. In this respect he is unlike the craftsman who seeks purely technical perfection with no concern for originality in design. The commercial lapidary, for instance, must become highly skilled in the use of mechanical equipment and processes in order to assure uniform results in the production of many identical items. Many amateurs and hobbyists proceed with this kind of mastery as their primary if not sole objective. While technical control is of the utmost importance in any artistic work, it should serve only as a means of expressing an aesthetic idea, not as an end in itself. The more mechanical technique becomes, the less artistic the end result.

Basic lapidary techniques can legitimately serve as formative steps in producing highly creative work. Some techniques, however, rely on automatic mechanical processes and practically exclude the creativity of the individual. These have either been eliminated altogether here or pointed in more original directions.

Basic techniques should be learned first, because the principles involved apply to even the most advanced work. These principles are not difficult to master: they can be learned by anyone with average aptitude and a desire to develop his ability. The basic techniques are sawing, grinding, sanding, polishing, and drilling. Most amateurs consider drilling a special technique, but since so much lapidary work of even the simplest kind requires it, the author has chosen to include it in this chapter.

Before attempting to cut a finished stone, you should become thoroughly acquainted with your tools and materials (3-1). The first step is to set up your equipment and learn how it functions. Read all the instructions that come with new machines. Be sure you understand the safety precautions and how to maintain your equipment in good working condition. Learn how to operate it by working with inexpensive materials. This will give you the feel of the machines and how the materials respond to them. Try materials with different degrees of hardness to see how they respond to sawing, grinding, sanding, and polishing. Try grinding different contours, cutting different shapes, making intersecting-angle cuts with the trim saw, using different grades of sanding cloth, different buffs and polishing compounds. With the sharp edge of the grinding wheel carve grooves on the face of a slab and notches in the edge. The idea is to be freely exploratory and experimental in your approach.

3-1.

47

Do not attempt to cut a finished stone in valuable material until you have gained some confidence and skill through this kind of practice. You may very well have some failures before you are able to produce results that will please you. Don't let this be a discouragement. Some individuals require more study and practice than others, but once the basic skills are mastered, anyone can produce creditable results.

When you are ready to attempt a finished stone, decide on the shape that you wish to cut. The beginner usually starts with a simple oval or round stone with a flat back and a rounded top, or *crown*. This is the easiest shape to master, and all the basic techniques except lapping and drilling are involved. Even drilling can be added if you want a hole to hang the stone, and finishing the flat back actually involves the principles of flat lapping on a small scale. This kind of stone, which can be almost any shape, is called a *cabochon* (3-2). The basic shape originated in ancient Egypt with the scarab (a kind of beetle), which had great religious and mystical significance and was one of the most popular decorative motifs for clothing and jewelry (see 5-4). It was carved in various materials such as turquoise, lapis lazuli, carnelian, chalcedony, and sardonyx and worn in rings by royalty and nobility. The scarab stone was set on a swivel pin, which allowed it to be turned over without removing it from the setting. The bottom side was carved with the seal of the wearer and served as his signet, or signature when pressed into a tablet of moist clay. When the seal was not in use, the rounded back of the scarab was worn uppermost. The scarab form was gradually simplified into a symmetrical oval stone with a rounded top. The swivel feature was retained, and the seal of the owner was still engraved on the bottom. Eventually the swivel was abandoned: the stone was set in a fixed bezel, or band of metal, and the seal was carved in the top. Finally the seal disappeared altogether, and the plain cabochon resulted. Cabochon stones were then admired and worn purely for their beauty and have been ever since.

The outline of a cabochon, as it appears from above, may be any shape whatever as long as the top is rounded (3-3). Certain shapes and dimensions have evolved that are strictly adhered to in commercial jewelry. The reason for this restrictive convention lies in the fact that lapidary and metalwork are separate industries in the commercial-jewelry trade. Mountings and settings are produced by the metal craftsman, but he does not know which stones may be used to fill them; similarly, stones are produced by the lapidary without any knowledge of which kind of mounting they may be set in. All that either craftsman needs to know are the standard shapes and

sizes that are used by the other. A commercial jeweler who supplies retailers may be little more than an assembler of stones and mountings procured from those who manufacture them.

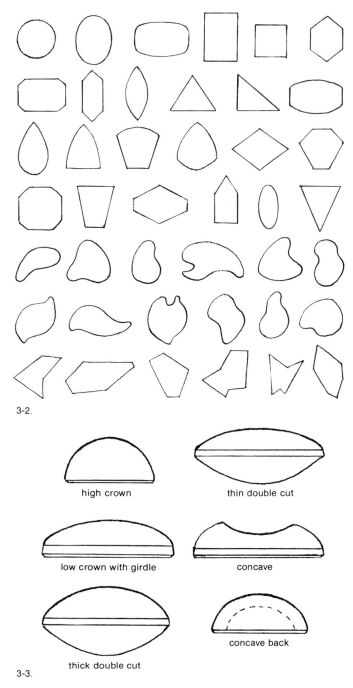

3-2.

high crown

thin double cut

low crown with girdle

concave

thick double cut

concave back

3-3.

48

To ensure that his stones will fit perfectly into manufactured mountings, the commercial lapidary uses templates of the standard shapes employed by the commercial metal craftsman. These are available in plastic sheets in which calibrated openings of standard shapes and sizes have been cut (3-4). Beginning lapidaries often use these same templates to mark stones for cutting. There is nothing particularly wrong with this procedure as a starting point, but many amateurs never venture any further: they seem to be unaware that more imaginative shapes can be cut to harmonize with the varying qualities of different materials or to become integral parts of a jewelry design. The creative lapidary uses templates only as a practice exercise to develop skill and accuracy, just as a beginning musician practices scales on his instrument. He is not content with cutting endless standard cabochons just to display his technical ability in this limited form.

Some amateurs deliberately cut their stones to standard patterns so that they will fit commercially available mountings. This is an attractive option to lapidaries who do no metalwork. It is an easy way to produce a complete piece of jewelry that one can wear, give to someone, or even sell. It shows off the work, even if it is only a part of the piece. But if you have a creative instinct and an artistic sense, it will never satisfy you. Commercial mountings are commonplace, since they are mechanically mass-produced. They are almost without exception poorly designed and in questionable taste. They can hardly be expected to lend distinction to any stone that is mounted in them.

Must the lapidary become a metalsmith in order to see his work properly mounted? Undeniably this is the best, most creative solution, the one that will achieve the best results and bring the most satisfaction. But the beginning lapidary may find this impossible, at least at the start. One suggestion is to work cooperatively with a good metal jeweler. If you can create the total design for a piece of jewelry, it is usually possible to find a jeweler who can reproduce it in metal and set the stone. Collaboration between lapidaries and metalsmiths, with either acting as the designer, has many possibilities, which have been almost completely ignored.

Regardless of your choice of shape and size for your cabochon, you have to prepare a blank of suitable material as a starting point. If you have a substantial piece of rough stone that you want to use, it must be sawed with a slabbing saw: you have to cut a slab that can be trimmed into a convenient blank for your stone.

Sawing
To use a slabbing saw, the rough piece is clamped in the vise so that the cut will be made at a selected spot. Depending on the type of material, the piece should be oriented to obtain the best color, optical effect, or pattern. Often a preliminary cut is necessary in order to determine the best orientation. If the piece is irregular in shape, it must be clamped securely to prevent any possibility of slipping or moving. Wooden wedges or shims can be inserted between the stone and the jaws of the vise (3-5). Sawed blocks of material with flat faces are easier to clamp, but they may also need shimming for

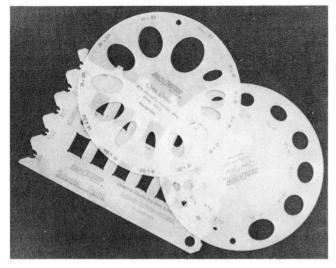

3-4.

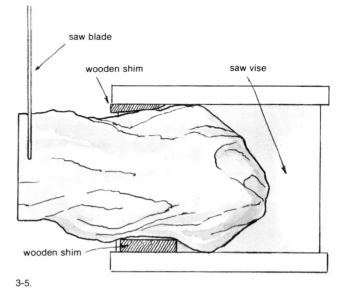

3-5.

proper alignment. Some rough pieces may need preliminary cuts on certain faces so that they can be clamped securely. The importance of secure clamping cannot be emphasized too much: if the rock should move out of line or slip during cutting, the saw blade can be damaged severely. Try to move the stone after it has been clamped in the vise. If you cannot move it, it should be safe, since the blade does not exert a great deal of pressure.

It is also very important to start the cut slowly and carefully so that the blade does not move out of line on initial contact with the rock. On some saws, particularly weight-feed models, it is possible to start the cut by hand. Automatic-feed saws can be adjusted to start the cut slowly, then increased to the proper rate. The following precautions should be observed at all times: never start the saw with the blade in contact with the stone; do not start the cut on a smooth surface that is not at right angles to the plane of the blade; never try to saw a mass of stone that is too large for the blade (the top of the blade should always extend above the top of the stone as it passes through); never operate the saw without enough fluid in the tank (it should extend about 1/2" on the bottom of the blade).

The various fluids, commonly called *coolants*, serve other purposes in addition to cooling. Their principal function is to flush the rock dust out of the cut as the blade wears it away. They also lubricate the cut, making it easier for the blade to rotate, and at the same time lubricate the other moving parts enclosed in the saw box. Since these parts are made of metal, the coolant must inhibit rust and corrosion; plain water will not do. The ideal coolant has good flushing action, lubricates both the cut and the saw parts, allows the rock dust to settle out rapidly, does not create fogging or misting, (fine mist in the area of the saw), is easily cleaned off the cut slabs, does not have an objectionable odor, is not too expensive, and is not dangerously flammable. None of the coolants currently available can provide all of these features. The traditional mixture is two or more parts of motor oil to ten of kerosene. Kerosene, however, has a penetrating odor that is objectionable to most people, and the oil is difficult to remove from the cut slabs, which means that the rock residue cannot settle out rapidly. Kerosene by itself would be better, but its flash point is dangerously low. The motor oil raises the flash point of the mixture to a safe level. There are now a number of products on the market that make excellent coolants in almost all respects; they are somewhat more expensive, but not much coolant is used up so that cost is not too great a consideration.

Most of these are known as *white oils*, *flushing oils*, or *light cutting oils* and are used in machine-shop work. Such products are made by most oil companies but sold wholesale only in 55-gallon drums. Some lapidary dealers stock and supply them to their patrons in small quantities. The different brands—Calube S 105 (Arco), Almag (Texaco), Pella 21 (Shell), and RPM Flushing Oil (Standard)—are similar to each other and more or less equal in performance. *Water-soluble* coolants are relatively expensive and leave a tenacious deposit on the blade and the rock-clamp track, which impedes the blade's rotation. This type of coolant is used to cut materials that may be altered by an oily solution, such as turquoise. Oily coolants can be used with these materials if the cut pieces are wiped off and immersed in a volatile solvent such as acetone, benzene, or alcohol; which will penetrate the stone and remove the oil.

In positioning the piece of material in the saw vise be sure to clamp it as close to one end as is practical: you may want to cut the entire piece into slabs without having to reclamp it. With the cross-feed arrangement on most slabbing saws consecutive slabs of any thickness can be cut right up to the jaws of the vise holding the stone. To make the first cut, move the stone in the vise to within a fraction of an inch of the saw blade. Start the motor. Move the vise forward slowly until the stone begins to contact the blade. After the blade has begun to cut into the rock, stop the saw and make sure that the cut is straight. If the blade has been pushed out of line by an irregularity on the face of the stone, move the piece slightly with the cross-feed setup.

The rate of feed should be adjusted to the kind of material and the size of the piece: the harder the material and the larger the size, the slower the rate of feed. This is a general rule, and precise adjustments are not mandatory. Fast speeds tend to wear out the saw blade; slow speeds may wear out your patience. The average pressure against the blade should be about 5 pounds for medium-hard materials such as agate. The *rate* of feed should average about 1" per 10 minutes. These estimates vary with the material, and precise instructions cannot be given. With experience you will have no difficulty in adjusting the rate of feed properly.

The rotary speed of the saw blade is more important. Manufacturers of diamond saw blades recommend a surface speed of 2,000' to 3,000' per minute. The pulleys that come with a slabbing saw run the blade at the proper speed. If you change the size of the pulleys, the blade, or the speed of the motor, a different peripheral speed will result. (Appendix 2 contains formulas and tables for calculating both surface speeds and revolutions per minute on most combinations of pulley and blade sizes and motor speeds. This information is especially important if you decide to build your own slabbing or trim saw.)

Once you have started the cut properly, the saw requires little attention, but it is a good idea to check progress from time to time. Unless your saw has an automatic cutoff, it is a good precaution to stop the saw with a fraction remaining to be cut and break off the slab by hand. This eliminates the possibility of a projecting spur of broken stone pushing the blade out of line as it feeds past. Slabs can be cut to exact thicknesses by turning the screw of the cross-feed. Determine the distance of one complete turn and count turns to obtain the proper thickness. The standard thickness of commercial gem-material slabs is 3/16". Some saws have vises that can only be adjusted by hand. The slab thicknesses can be set by measuring the distance from the blade to the outer edge of the stone in the vise. This edge may be so irregular that it will have to be trimmed in order to get a smooth surface to start from. The first slab can be used to measure and set the thickness of succeeding slabs. By placing this slab flat against the blade you can line up the outer faces of the stone in the vise correctly. The next cut will yield a slab of the same thickness (3-6).

When the slab is sawed and cleaned, mark the outline of the cabochon stone on the surface with a template and a marking point. Templates for standard shapes and sizes are usually made of plastic with openings for the exact outlines of the different cuts. The marker can be an aluminum nail or bronze rod sharpened to a fine point. This shows up well on all but very light materials; for these waterproof felt-tipped marking pens are excellent. Hard crayon pencils can also be used. Select the best area of the slab for your stone; lay the template over it and mark the outline (3-7).

To design your own shapes, you have to make your own templates. Draw the outline on a thin sheet of plastic or metal and saw it out with a jeweler's saw. You can use either the opening or the cutout solid piece. If you are skilled at drawing, you may be able to dispense with a template altogether and draw the outline directly on the stone blank. If you want to cut a pair of matching asymmetrical stones, mark one blank, then turn the template over to mark the other. The two stones will be mirror images of each other.

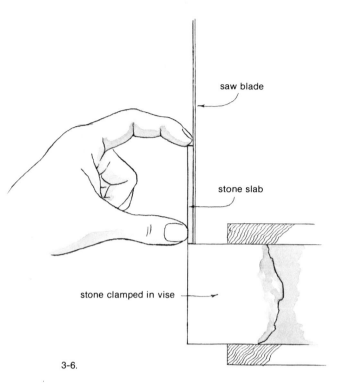

3-6.

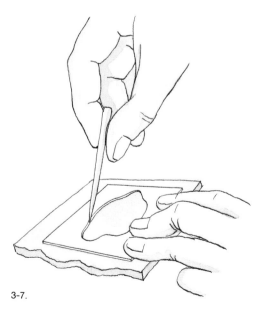

3-7.

With the trim saw cut the blank out of the slab with as many straight cuts as necessary. Rest the slab flat on the table, push it forward in a straight line, start the cut slowly, and push just hard enough to hold the slab in firm contact with the blade. Too much force tears the diamond grit out of the metal. If the cutout area is some distance from the edge of the slab, mark straight lines for the cuts (3-8): without guidelines you may cut into the outline of the stone.

A great deal of skill can be developed with the trim saw. The sharp points that are left by the long, straight initial cuts can be trimmed off with multiple short cuts until there is very little material left to be ground away. On relatively hard materials such as agate and jasper, these projections can be nibbled off with a pair of stout pliers; softer materials or materials with weak cleavage may break in the wrong place. A guiderail on the trim-saw table is very handy for parallel straight cuts; if your saw does not have this feature, it is not difficult to install a homemade guide (see chapter 2).

Unlike the slabbing saw, most trim saws can be used with plain water as a coolant. No feeding mechanism is contained in the tank, so rust and corrosion are not a problem. A rust inhibitor should be added to the water, however, particularly if a slabbing vise is attached to the saw. Steel parts should be protected with a coating of cup grease, whether or not a rust inhibitor is used.

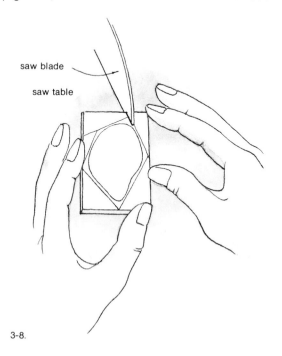

saw blade

saw table

3-8.

Trim saws that do not have a vise can be used to cut small pebbles or fragments. Hold them firmly and push in a straight line against the blade. Do not allow the stone to twist out of line, or it will be grabbed by the blade, which may break the stone and damage the blade. If the stone does not have a fairly flat side that can be rested against the table while sawing, one should be ground to avoid unconsciously tipping the stone out of line with the blade. For the same reason any projections left by the slab saw should be trimmed or ground off to allow the slab to lie perfectly flat while trimming.

Grinding

After the blank for the cabochon has been trimmed, the next step is to grind it into shape. If it is large enough to hold comfortably with the fingers, do not mount it on a dop stick, as for sanding and polishing. Better control is possible without the rigid stick. The beginner should be cautious, however, because it is very easy to grind your fingers. If you are apprehensive, put the stone on a stick until you feel more confident.

The process of *dopping* consists of fastening the stone on a *dop stick* with *dopping wax*, a mixture of sealing wax and flake or stick shellac pressed into square sticks for convenient use. It is inexpensive and can be used over and over. Dop sticks are usually pieces of wooden dowel rods cut to convenient lengths of 3″ or 4″ and in diameters from 1/8 to 1″. Round handles from small, worn-out artist's brushes, pen holders, etc., can also be used, as well as wooden matchsticks or round toothpicks for very tiny stones. The diameter of the stick should be somewhat less than that of the stone. The wax is melted, usually over an alcohol lamp, by holding the wax stick in the flame. When the wax is soft, a small amount is applied to the end of the dop stick. The stone is held briefly in the flame with tweezers until it is fairly warm. The wax on the stick is remelted and quickly applied to the surface of the stone, which will adhere and remain in position on the stick (3-9). While it is soft, the wax can be molded with moistened fingers to the proper shape to support the stone; a soldering torch, adjusted to a soft flame, can also be used for this operation. The stone is laid on a heat-resistant surface (a soldering pad or sheet of asbestos) and heated simultaneously with the wax on the end of the dop stick. The stone should be perpendicular to the stick, not tilted (3-10). Some lapidaries use an electric wax pot to keep the wax at just the right temperature (3-11). This is not practical unless you habitually do large numbers of cabochons at a time. If you do only a few stones intermittently, the pot has to be reheated each time, which takes 30 minutes. If the pot is left on for several hours, the wax will dry out and become brittle.

The purpose of grinding is to shape the stone accurately. Although sanding is used to remove very minor irregularities left on the surface, the grinder must shape the stone in its final contours: flat spots of any size left on the surface cannot be easily removed by sanding unless you are working with very soft materials (under 6 in hardness). Some softer materials can be shaped entirely by sanding. A continuous flood of water over the surface of the wheel is necessary to keep the stone from overheating and to flush away the ground-off material, which would soon clog the pores of the wheel (see chapter 2).

If a horizontal grinder is used, sit in a comfortable position in front of the wheel. You may have to experiment with different seat or bench heights to find a comfortable position. If you use a vertical grinder, your relation to the wheel will be somewhat different. Freedom of movement is more restricted.

Before you start grinding, make sure that the wheels are set to run at the proper speed. They will have a notation on the blotter pad stating the maximum speed at which they should be operated: *don't exceed this speed*. Refer to the formulas or the speed tables in appendix 2 to be sure that your wheels run between 4,000 and 6,000 s.f.m. (surface feet per minute).

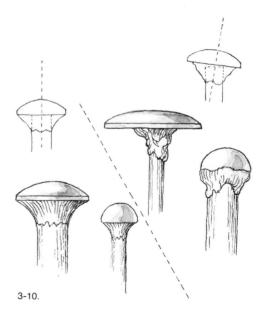

3-10.

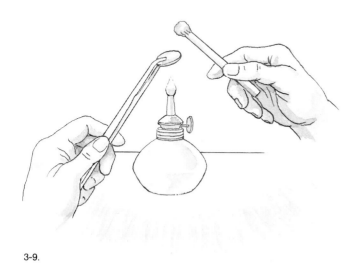

3-9.

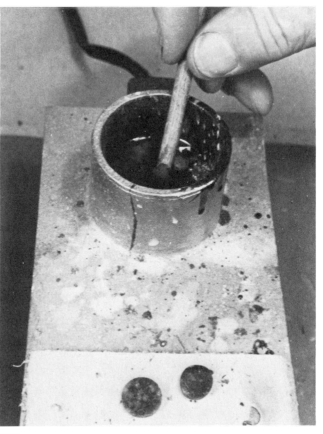

3-11.

If you grind without a dop stick, you will soon develop your own method of holding the stone. The author's method is to place the back of the stone on the forefinger of the left hand and to grasp the stone by the edges with the tips of the thumb and the second finger of the right hand. The stone is controlled with these fingers, while it is rotated and swung from side to side on the finger of the left hand (3-12). A dop stick is held in both hands. It is rotated and swung in an arc in order to cover the entire surface of the stone in successive steps from the outer edge to the center.

Whether you are using a stick or not, the procedure is the same (3-13): begin by grinding a domed or curved top on the stone, starting around the outer edge, grind a bevel all the way around to within 1mm or 2mm of the edge, and grind successive bevels in this manner until you come almost to the top of the crown (1). Work across the ridges left between the bevels by rocking the stone as you move it across the grinder. Grind the rounded top before the outline (2): a thin edge is easier to grind to a perfect outline (3), whereas if the edge is the full thickness of the blank, it is more difficult to control, it takes longer to grind, and there is more wear on the surface of the wheel (4). Many lapidaries follow the opposite sequence, but it takes no longer to grind the top down to the approximate girdle to start with than to first complete the final girdle, and with the former method the final outline (leaving a small margin for sanding) is quickly and accurately achieved by grinding the much thinner edge. The final grinding of the top is then accomplished to leave a precise border, or girdle, of the same height all around the stone. This girdle will be relatively proportional in width to the size and thickness of the stone. It should have a slight slope of 5° to 10° inward toward the top: this angle is very important if the stone is to be set in a *bezel*, a metal band that encircles the stone. In setting the stone the jeweler forces and compresses the bezel inward against the girdle. Since the stone is fitted into a band that is smaller at the top than at the bottom, or base, it is held securely in place.

Some stones with high crowns are not cut with a girdle: the steep slope of the sides furnishes the angle against which the bezel is burnished (3-3:1). In either case the stone can be set with prongs to hold it in place instead of a bezel. On all stones with flat backs an acute angle is created where the top meets the back. It should be removed by grinding a very small beveled edge (3-13), which tends to prevent chipping of the otherwise acute edge.

Always move the stone constantly *across* the face of the grinding wheel, not up and down. This wears the wheel evenly, keeping the face flat and square, and avoids developing grooves and flat spots that will bump the stone. Moving the stone rapidly back and forth and rotating it at the same time prevents flat spots from developing on the cabochon. Constantly check for symmetry by holding the stone up to eye level against a light background to show the curve of the top. Look at the side of the stone, then take an end view. Although

3-12.

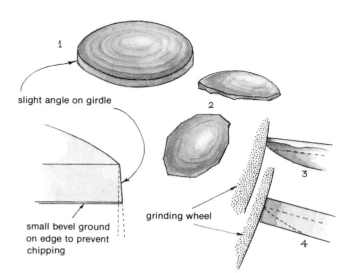

1

slight angle on girdle

2

3

small bevel ground on edge to prevent chipping

grinding wheel

4

3-13.

it will not be a perfectly smooth line, the curve from both viewpoints should be symmetrical without breaks or angles. Practice to develop a light touch. It is not necessary to press hard: this only wears the wheel more rapidly without hastening the work. This principle applies to all grinding, sawing, and drilling operations.

Most beginners have some difficulty in producing an evenly ground surface; with the first sanding flat spots may appear, and the stone may have to be reground to achieve a more even surface. Use a magnifier if necessary to locate the flat spots. One of the reasons for using a coarse and a fine wheel successively is that it is easier to produce an even surface on a slower-cutting wheel. There will be tiny flat planes all over even the smoothest surface, but these are easily removed by the sweeping, brushing motions in sanding, which cover the whole surface evenly. Only the larger flats that are not removed easily by sanding must be eliminated by doing a more perfect job of grinding.

Even though your grinding technique may be perfect as far as moving the work evenly across the wheel is concerned, flat spots will eventually develop and the wheel will start to bump. The wheel must then be *dressed* to restore its smoothness, or it will become virtually unusable. It is best to dress the wheel when you first feel the effects of a flat spot: this allows smoother grinding and avoids a lengthy and difficult job of dressing the surface evenly later. Wheel dressers are of three general types, diamond, star, or a simple bar or block of coarse, hard-bond silicon carbide. The latter type is not very efficient and is not recommended.

With a steady rest set just below the center of the wheel the dresser is passed slowly across the entire face, removing a very small amount of material each time and continuing until all the irregularities are removed. Star and bar diamond dressers must slide across the rest from side to side; single-point or cluster diamond dressers mounted on round rods can be rolled along the rest to assure that contact remains on the same plane for each movement. A certain amount of skill is required to dress the wheel properly without removing more material than necessary. To assist in the operation, there are several types of jig blocks that hold the diamond dresser on a metal platform in alignment with the wheel face and also allow the depth of the cut to be set and maintained.

Sanding

When you are satisfied that the stone has been properly ground, proceed to the sander. The sanding technique is rather different from that of grinding. All stones except very large slabs should be mounted on dop sticks,

and even large stones that can be easily held with the fingers are best dopped, particularly for dry sanding, which generates a considerable amount of heat and makes the stone uncomfortably hot. Because of the sweeping, rotating movements used in either type of sanding you will have greater control and maneuverability if the stone has a handle—which is provided by the dop stick.

Start sanding by stroking the stone against the sander with a sweeping, up-and-down movement. Try to cover a large surface area with each stroke, which will remove the tiny facets left by the grinder and leave a smooth, even contour. The same technique is used for both wet and dry sanding. Begin with a coarse-grit cloth and progress to medium, fine, and ultrafine: suggested grit sizes are, respectively, 120, 220, 320, and 600. Some lapidaries eliminate the ultrafine cloth by using a very well-worn 320 cloth as the last prepolish stage. This produces a fairly high luster on most gem materials.

Wet sanding is faster than dry sanding. Be careful not to oversand in the first stages with a new cloth: the shape of the stone can be changed unintentionally, particularly with softer materials. Final cutting of the girdle is often done better on the coarse or even the medium sander than on the fine grinding wheel.

In the successive stages of sanding the scratches left by the previous stage must be completely removed by the next: the surface becomes smoother with each stage until it attains a perfectly even prepolish—that is, an even gloss. Examine the surface of the stone carefully before moving to the next stage: deeper scratches left by the previous stage will show up later, and you will have to backtrack to a coarser cloth to remove them. Use a magnifier if necessary to check.

There are advantages to both wet and dry sanding. The wet-or-dry cloth used for wet sanding is substantially more expensive than dry cloth, but it lasts a great deal longer. Water keeps the cloth clean, and the work cool. If the stone is on a dop stick, the wax remains hard, and the stone will not come off from overheating, as in dry sanding. Some stones such as opal are *heat sensitive* to *burning*—a whitening or other discoloration due to overheating—cracking, or crazing, dangers that wet sanding avoids. On the other hand, some materials such as nephrite jades seem to work better with dry sanding, and a good prepolish in the author's opinion is easier to achieve on some softer stones, although wet sanding is currently the preferred technique.

Dry-sanding cloth will eventually lose its efficiency, but it can easily be renewed. Dust the surface of the cloth thoroughly with a cheap 2" paintbrush with short bristles, removing as much of the embedded material as possible, then dip the brush in water and wet the entire surface. Let the wheel stand for a few seconds to soften the glue holding the grit to the cloth, then scrub the surface with the brush to loosen the remaining dust. When the glue begins to smear, stroke the surface lightly and evenly all around the wheel. The loosened grit will be displaced and turned over so that sharp new facets will be uppermost. When the cloth is completely dry, it will cut like new, and the surface can be renewed several times before discarding.

Most lapidaries, particularly hobbyists who cut nothing but cabochons, use sanders with a soft backing, either sponge rubber or soft felt. This is fine for rounded forms but not for flat surfaces: they will become rounded on the edges, and the center will not be sanded at all. Expandable drums have the same effect. Soft backings are also unsatisfactory for materials that vary in hardness: the soft areas tend to undercut and leave an irregular texture that cannot be polished successfully. Nephrite and jadeite, rhodonite, lapis lazuli, and some agates and jaspers are typical examples of such materials. For general work on a variety of surfaces and contours a layer of cork under the cloth offers a surface that is just firm enough. Although softer backings are easier for the beginner to manipulate, many more shapes and materials can be sanded on a firmer backing. The edge of the drum sander can be used to work into shallow curves, channels, and other irregularities in carvings, both small and large. This edge can also be used effectively to sand flat areas such as the backs of stones, which are difficult to reach with the broader surface of the wheel. The sharp edge of the cork should be slightly rounded by holding a piece of medium-grit sanding cloth against it while it is running. The edge of the mounted sanding-cloth belt will conform to this curve when the work is pressed against it (3-14).

With a disk sander the stone is manipulated in a slightly different manner, because the flat side of the wheel is used rather than its peripheral face. The surface speed is fastest at the outer edge of the wheel and decreases toward the center. For this reason most sanding should be done on the outer half of the disk. A disk sander with a slight crown is better than one that is perfectly flat, because the former allows good contact in the center of a flat surface. For rounded contours a disk with a soft backing or no backing allows the cloth to conform to the surface and makes the work a bit easier.

A vertical-belt sander offers a variety of surfaces: flat, round-drum, resilient, and firm. Work can be done on the surface of the round lower pulley, which has a firm rubber backing, or on the area between the two drums, which by itself is soft and resilient; firm and flat, if the back plate is installed.

In sanding as in other lapidary processes the speed of the machine is important: the surface speed should be between 2,000' and 3,000' per minute for most materials. Slower speeds wear the cloth excessively, because greater pressure is used to accomplish the same results. Speed requirements for wet or dry sanding are the same.

Materials that vary in texture or hardness are difficult to sand and polish. They tend to *undercut*—the softer material is cut away faster than the harder, leaving a roughened or pitted surface. Stones that have inclusions of softer material, such as spots of *matrix* (mother rock), are particularly susceptible to unevenness of finish. Some materials contain soft areas that cannot possibly be given an even, high polish. In such cases a decision has to be made: either to discard the stone or to incorporate it into a design in which the uneven texture becomes unobjectionable or even enhances the total effect. An imperfect stone that has no value on the commercial-gem market may have a high artistic value if it is used in a creative way. Many of these problem stones can be finished successfully by applying special sanding techniques. For wet sanding a new, sharp cloth should be used with plenty of water. The water acts as a protective film for the softer parts while the harder areas are being cut down. If this procedure is followed through all sanding stages, polishing may be much easier. In dry sanding somewhat slower speeds seem to give better results on undercutting materials. Use light pressure until the final prepolish stage, then heavier pressure to develop an even gloss.

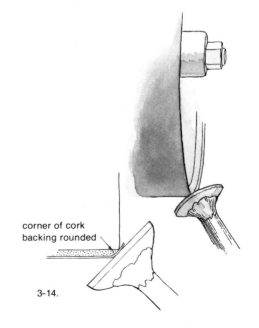

corner of cork
backing rounded

3-14.

Other materials besides regular sanding cloth will produce good results. Leather, used as a belt or as a disk, is very effective for fine sanding. A thin, wet mixture of grits from 400 to 1,200 is brushed on the leather surface, which should be slightly damp for sanding. Much slower speeds must be used to prevent the grit mixture from being thrown off the surface. The leather should be fairly thin and smooth (but not slick) and mounted on a firm backing. With very fine abrasive grit, 1,200 or 1,400, this technique is often the answer to undercutting problems. Wooden wheels and abrasive grit can also be used for sanding. Cylinders of grit in a number of grades, compressed with a binder into a tube of heavy paper, are commercially available. The compound is water-soluble. The wheel or belt is moistened, and the open end of the bar is applied to the surface while the machine is running. These convenient bars are also available in different polishing compounds for wheels and belts.

Polishing

Diamond compounds can be used on leather or wood wheels for both sanding and polishing. Application of the compound to the surface is different than with silicon-carbide grits: the diamond particles are embedded and *charge* the wheel. This charge is retained for a considerable period. The diamond grit is mixed with a greasy or oily substance and rubbed on the surface by hand. Small wheels (3″ or 4″) are usually used, and grits range from 325, to 600, 1,200, 3,000, 8,000, and 14,000 in succession, which sands and polishes most materials. Grits as high as 50,000 (1 micron) or even 100,000 are sometimes used for a high polish. The diamond grit is mixed with the carrier to a spreadable consistency, using as much diamond as possible. Graded grit is available in dry powder form or premixed to the proper consistency in handy syringes. A separate wheel must be used for each grade of grit. Hardwood wheels (maple is excellent) are best for working very hard stones such as corundum (ruby and sapphire), chrysoberyl, and emerald, as well as softer materials. It is more difficult to avoid flats in the sanding stage with hardwood than with leather wheels, but polishing is no problem if the sanding is done properly.

Polishing techniques vary considerably for different types of materials, and experience is the best guide. With thorough sanding polishing should require only a few minutes for most average-size stones, but some materials polish more easily than others. If you are a beginner, choose a cryptocrystalline material, such as solid agate, jasper, carnelian, or bloodstone, for your first cabochon. If it is solid with no soft inclusions, it should polish easily on a felt buff with tin oxide or cerium oxide.

Leave your stone cemented to the dop stick. Wash it in clean water to remove any grit remaining from sanding. Mix the polishing material to a creamy consistency and apply it to the buffing wheel with a 1″ to 2″ paintbrush, letting it soak into the felt. Do not start the machine until the surface is practically dry. The wheel should revolve at a fairly slow speed (between 1,000 and 2,000 s.f.m.). If the buff becomes too dry, remoisten it by holding the loaded brush against it while it is running. At the slow speed the mixture will not be thrown off the buff. Test the surface with your finger. When it is moist but not wet, press the stone against it and slowly rotate it so that all parts of the surface are contacted. You will feel the buff begin to pull against the stone; great heat is generated at the minute point of heaviest contact. Microphotographs show that the surface actually flows over and bridges the microscopic scratches left by the final sanding. If the scratches are too deep, the surface will flow into them, resulting in a polish with a wavy rather than an even surface. The intense heat that causes the flow of the surface is not immediately transmitted throughout the mass of the stone. If the stone is not held too long against the buff, it will not become hot enough to cause the surface to burn or the dop wax to melt. A technique of intermittent pressure and removal will avoid this danger. Use a magnifier to make sure that all parts of the surface are polished to perfection, including the back (except for opaque stones that will be mounted in a closed setting). All translucent stones should have a polished back, whether it will be seen or not, so that transmission of light through the material will be unobstructed. After the top is finished, reverse the stone on the dop stick and sand and polish the back.

To remove the stone from the dop stick, either heat it until the wax is soft and twist it off, knock it off (3-15), or

3-15.

put it in the refrigerator or in a pan of ice water for several minutes. It will detach itself cleanly, because the change of temperature causes the wax to shrink. The third procedure is the cleanest, but it takes more time. With the other two methods some wax is always left on the stone. It can be removed by heating it and scraping away the softened wax with a dull knife blade. To eliminate all traces, soak the stone in alcohol for a few minutes and wipe clean. If you knock the stone off the dop stick, be sure to use a wooden mallet or stick and place a cloth under the block to catch the stone to avoid damage. Do not use this method on fragile materials.

Lapping

Lapping refers to the grinding, sanding, and polishing of flat surfaces. The lapping machines described in chapter 2 are all designed to achieve the same effect, but different techniques are used for each. Automatic or semiautomatic lapping machines require little skill or attention from the operator. But the standard flat, horizontal lap (2-27) which has been used for hundreds of years, depends on careful handwork to produce satisfactory results. Lapping with abrasive grit is somewhat different from grinding with a solid abrasive wheel. The abrasive grains roll between the lap plate and the face of the stone, which produces a pitted rather than scratched surface. Successively finer grains make the pits finer and finer until an evenly frosted, semipolished surface is achieved. For best results the final polishing should be done on the appropriate polishing buff for the material involved.

To prepare the lap machine, line the pan with paper—newspaper will do—to catch any grit that may splash into the pan. Each time the grits are changed, a new liner should be put in to avoid contaminating a slab with coarser grit if it is dropped acidentally into the pan. The grits normally used are: 220 for the first lapping, 400 for the next, and 1,200 for the final stage. The grit is mixed with water to form a rather sloppy slurry and brushed on the lap plate with a different brush for each grade of abrasive. The mixture should not be too liquid or applied in too thick a layer, because the excess will be thrown off the edges of the plate and wasted. The consistency should resemble thin mud. For the last stage the mixture should be very thin, not like a paste. A very small amount of detergent added to the mixture helps it to spread evenly.

Check the piece to be lapped to be sure that there are no projections that will prevent it from lying flat. These must be ground off before starting. Place the piece on the lap, hold it down, and start the machine. As the lap rotates, sweep the piece back and forth across the entire diameter of the plate. If you lap only on the outer half of the plate, it will eventually wear out, making the plate uneven, and it will then have to be resurfaced.

If the piece has been smoothly cut with a good slabbing saw, lapping with the coarse grit will be minimized. But you must always make sure that a perfectly flat, smooth surface has been achieved before moving to the next stage. Wash the grit off the slab from time to time and inspect the piece. Let the light fall at an angle across the surface to show up any low areas. These are not difficult to see in the first stage, because the unlapped areas contrast markedly with the rest of the surface, but in the intermediate and fine stages you have to look more closely. A good way to discover low spots is to mark the surface with closely spaced crossing lines—use a good waterproof marker, a felt-tip pen, or an aluminum point. When you relap the surface, untouched spots will be clearly visible: just continue lapping until no marks remain.

After each lapping the plate, the piece, and your hands must be washed off carefully to remove every trace of grit. Use a stiff brush on the lap to assure a thorough job. The lap should be kept wet constantly. A container of water set above the wheel, with a valve that can be adjusted to a slow drip, is helpful. Grit must also be added with the brush from time to time. In lapping thin slabs a backing of some sort makes it easier to hold the slab and manipulate it. It can be a section of a thin board or a thicker slab of gem material. Attach it with a few spots of dopping wax, which are easily removed by heating.

The vibrating lap (2-29), a comparatively recent invention, can save a lot of time and labor. The lapping action is entirely automatic: the operator need only change and add grits occasionally as the work progresses. The polishing pad furnished with this machine achieves an excellent final finish. This lap can also accommodate several pieces at a time, another big timesaver. The edges should be protected from chipping by surrounding them with heavy rubber bands or rubber tubing. Lightweight pieces should be weighted to speed up lapping and polishing action. The same grit sequence can be used as with the hand lap, but some machines have special recommendations that it is best to follow.

In using the overhead, or overarm, oscillating lap (2-28) one or more stone slabs are fastened to the table of the machine. The grit mixture is applied to the face of the work, then the runner—a metal plate—is brought into contact with the stone and oscillated across it in a sweeping motion. Unlike the horizontal lap, different plates can be attached to the arm and used for each grit, which eliminates the necessity of washing the plate each time the grit is changed. Polishing pads are attached in the same way. Since a lot of downward pressure can be exerted on the arm, polishing as well as other operations is somewhat faster than with the standard flat lap, and a number of slabs can be worked at the same time.

The slabs are laid face down on a smooth, level surface. A light wooden frame is placed around them, and plaster of paris is poured into the frame, covering the slabs (3-16). When the plaster hardens, the block is turned over and fastened securely to the table of the machine. It can then be surfaced as if it were a block of solid material. Since the arm of this machine can be swung over a wide area, large pieces such as tabletops can be surfaced (see chapter 5).

3-16.

Drilling

Most methods of drilling hard gem materials are relatively slow. Although recently developed drilling machines utilizing ultrasonic and laser beams are extremely fast, the cost of such equipment makes it feasible only for commercial volume drilling. The professional craftsman who does a significant amount of drilling needs a machine that raises and lowers either the drill or the work automatically. An automatic drill is operated in the same manner as a hand drill, but there are precautions to be observed. Unless the automatic mechanism allows gentle contact between the drill bit and the stone (some do), solid diamond-impregnated bits should not be used: they are too fragile to endure the thumping action. Do not allow the drill bit to complete the hole: the last fraction of an inch should either be finished by hand feeding or by turning the stone over and completing the hole from the other side to avoid chipping brittle materials.

The method to use for drilling small holes depends on the material and the equipment. The different methods are: solid diamond-impregnated or -plated bits, lubricated with water; diamond-chip-embedded bits, used with water; metal tube drills, used with diamond grit in oil; metal tube drills, used with silicon-carbide grit in water; solid iron or steel bits, used with diamond grit in oil; solid iron or steel bits, used with silicon-carbide grit in water; solid tungsten-carbide twist drills, used in water; and solid steel twist drills, used in water.

With solid diamond-impregnated drills, plated-diamond drills, and diamond-chip-embedded drills the stone should be immersed in water during drilling. All drilling methods require a machine that is capable of intermittent raising and lowering of the drill or the table. One convenient arrangement that can be used with most miniature drill presses and drilling machines is to install a shallow pan on the table. It can be held in place with a clamp or clamps or cemented to the table as a permanent or semipermanent installation.

To seat the stone for drilling, heat the bottom of the pan with a torch and apply a small amount of dopping wax or paraffin. The latter is easier to remove. Heat the stone and the wax and set the stone in the wax under the drill point. While the wax is soft, the stone can be positioned exactly for the drill to make the hole. Heat heat-sensitive materials with a soft, low flame. Do not use modeling clay to fasten the stone: it may shift in this soft material.

If the stone is already polished, grind a spot for the drill to start on, particularly if the surface is sloped. This can be done with a small diamond or silicon-carbide burr. The roughened surface will prevent the drill from slipping out of line and breaking. The danger is not so great with unpolished stones, but with polishing after drilling the sharp edges of the hole will bite into the polishing buff. This can be minimized by countersinking or beveling the edges of the hole with a tapered-cone silicon-carbide point or a regular diamond hole-beveler point.

After the stone is cemented in place, fill the pan with water to just cover the top of the stone. Start the motor and run it at moderate speed. If you are using a drill press with a knob control, gradually raise the table until the drill contacts the stone very lightly. Exert as little pressure as possible while the bit is grinding a seat for itself; then you can run the drill at full speed. Always use just enough pressure to keep the drill in firm contact with the stone. Too much pressure will tear the diamond particles out of the bond.

If you are using a drill with a knob that lowers the table, break contact at 5- or 6-second intervals while drilling to allow water to run into the hole and flush out the ground material (3-17). If you attempt to drill dry, dust will build up in the hole and stop the cutting action, and the drill and the stone will become hot and crack the stone. The same method is used for machines with a handle that lowers the drill. The first type allows more sensitive hand control.

When the hole is almost finished, use an absolute minimum of pressure to avoid chipping the edges as the point of the drill breaks through. With some tough stones such as jade there is very little danger of chipping, but with even slightly brittle stones it is safest to stop drilling before the bottom is reached. Pour the water out of the pan and remove the stone by heating it until the wax softens. Solder a pin the same diameter as the drill vertically to a small, flat metal base. Cut the pin off to a length just slightly shorter than the hole is deep. Cement the metal plate holding the pin with dop wax to the bottom of the pan, with the pin lined up so that the point of the drill is exactly centered above it (3-18). Turn the stone over with the base up and mount by inserting

the pin in the hole. Use a little dop wax under the stone to secure it in place, but be careful not to move the pin out of position while the wax is soft. You can now complete the hole from the back with the assurance that the drill will intersect perfectly with the front hole.

Solid diamond-impregnated bits do not drill materials above 7 on the Mohs' scale very rapidly because of the *dead center* in the solid, rotating point. Nephrite jade drills very easily, but cryptocrystalline-quartz materials such as agate and jasper take time. Speeds higher than 5,000 r.p.m. are helpful. For some unknown reason manufacturers of these drills recommend relatively slow speeds (under 10,000 r.p.m.), but higher speeds are obviously more efficient.

With light pressure and high speed there is less wear on the bit, and the work is accomplished much more rapidly than at slower speeds.

If the drill you are using is mounted on a vertical column with set screws, be sure that these are securely tightened, or the machine may drift out of line while operating, jam the bit in the hole, and break it. Drills can also be broken by striking them accidentally while they are mounted in the chuck or by dropping them. The smaller sizes are especially fragile. Using a hand-held machine with this type of drill is not to be recommended under any circumstances. A small, sensitive drill press is a necessity for drilling accurate holes in hard materials.

If you are drilling harder materials or deep holes, which take some time, an automatic device that lifts the drill or lowers the table is a great convenience and time-saver (3-19). As mentioned previously, smaller diamond-impregnated drills and homemade diamond-chip drills should not be used with this device unless it returns the drill to the hole very gently. It is safest to drill these by hand control, as they are extremely fragile.

3-17.

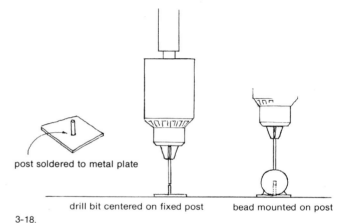

post soldered to metal plate

drill bit centered on fixed post   bead mounted on post

3-18.

Tube drills used with diamond abrasive offer a reasonably fast means of drilling holes of any size, from very small up to the diameter of the largest tube that the chuck or collet of the miniature drill press can hold. In cutting the tube to the proper length be sure that the drilling end is square with the axis of the tube. A piece of rivet wire or rod the same diameter as the hole in the tube can be fitted into the section that goes in the chuck so that the tube cannot distort or collapse when the jaws of the chuck are tightened. If this core is not used, tighten the chuck just enough to hold the tube firmly. Some authorities recommend *upsetting*, or slightly flaring the cutting end of the tube, to provide clearance for the shank. This is not really necessary, as some of the particles of grit will work around the outer wall of the tube, and the hole will be drilled slightly larger than the diameter of the tube. The hole will be slightly smaller at the bottom than at the top because of the wearing action of the grit on the outer wall of the tube.

The stone must be fastened down as in drilling with solid bits, but since this type of drilling is not done underwater, the pan can be removed from the table. A flat piece of wood or Masonite should be cemented or clamped to the table as a base for the stone. A small reservoir around the spot for the hole is necessary to contain the grit mixture (3-20). If the stone is flat, a short section of tubular material or even a flat washer can be cemented down with dop wax or paraffin. On irregular surfaces or for holes near the edge of the stone the reservoir must be made of some workable material that will adhere to the stone and base. The author has found the hard carving wax used by lost-wax casters to be ideal for this purpose.

3-19. The arrow points to a cam arm on the shaft of a slow-r.p.m. motor, which turns the wheel and is fastened to a knob control. The spring intermittently lowers the pan and returns it to the drill bit.

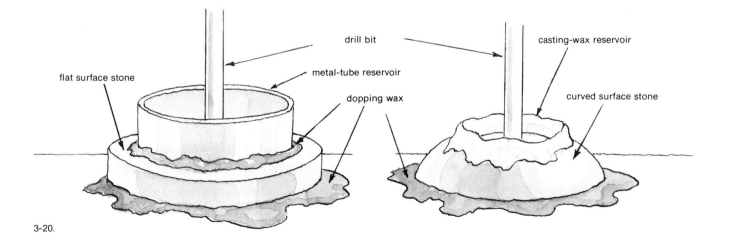

flat surface stone

drill bit

metal-tube reservoir

dopping wax

casting-wax reservoir

curved surface stone

3-20.

If the stone and the base are only slightly warm, the hot wax will adhere firmly. The walls of the reservoir can be easily built up with a regular waxing tool or any metal point that will drip hot wax. Paraffin can be used for this purpose, but the walls are more difficult to build up than with the hard wax. Plasticine modeling clay is easier to apply, but it is difficult to salvage the valuable diamond grit. The grains are embedded in the clay, and it is almost impossible to separate them. They can be flushed off the hard wax with kerosene and poured into a small container. They will settle to the bottom, and the kerosene can be drained off, leaving the grit to be reused.

When you are ready to drill, pour a few drops of light-weight machine oil in the reservoir. With a toothpick dipped in oil pick up a small amount of diamond grit and add it to the oil in the reservoir. For most drilling 200 grit is best, but 400 is better for very small holes. Drill for a few seconds, then raise the drill to allow the grit and oil to run to the bottom of the hole. The grit will be partially embedded in the bottom edge of the tube and do the cutting. This action can be assisted by sawing very fine notches in the end. As the cutting proceeds downward, a core of the material will rise inside the tube. This core has a tendency to break off and jam in the tube, especially in small drills and with comparatively soft, fragile materials. It must be removed before drilling can continue. It can usually be pushed out with a wire, but it is easier to watch the drilling closely and break the cores off in the hole. They can be removed with sticky wax on the end of a toothpick. Tube drills should be operated at much slower speeds than solid diamond drills. They cut faster because much less material has to be ground away, and there is no dead center. Speeds from 2,000 to 3,000 r.p.m. are used for drills up to 1/8" in diameter; the speed should be reduced as the diameter increases.

Tube drills used with silicon-carbide abrasive are operated in the same manner as with diamond grit except that the grit is mixed with water instead of oil. The same kinds of tubes are used, but two to four rather deep slots should be sawed vertically in the cutting end to allow the abrasive mixture to flow freely around and under the edge of the bit.

Solid metal bits can also be used with either diamond or silicon-carbide grit. The technique is the same as with tube drilling but considerably slower. Hard-drawn brass or nickel-silver rivet wire or the shanks of small nails can be used. The drill should be perfectly straight. It can be straightened in the chuck by bending carefully with jeweler's pliers. If it is still not straight or concentric, it can be trued up with a small, flat file, held flat against it as it rotates in the chuck. File down the shank in this way until

it is slightly smaller than a short section on the cutting end. The larger diameter of the point will cut clearance for the smaller shank. For better cutting with solid drills saw shallow crossing slots in the bottom of the cutting edge; these tend to hold the grit under the point.

Very small holes can be drilled in hard materials (7 and above) with steel needles. The procedure is the same as for larger holes using either solid or tube metal drills with a mixture of diamond grit. The only difference is that an automatic machine is practically a necessity because the drilling rate is very slow, especially with very hard materials (8 to 9 on the Mohs' scale). The drill should be set and the hole started by hand before connecting the automatic device. There is no need for the return to be gentle, as a forceful contact tends to embed the diamond in the face of the drill. No attention is needed except to add some mixture (diamond grit in oil) as required. Medium speeds from 1,000 to 2,000 r.p.m. are most practical. Steel twist drills can be used on gem materials under 5 in hardness, and most materials under 6 1/2 in hardness can be drilled successfully with tungsten-carbide drills, which usually cost less than half as much as equivalent-size diamond drills. It is best to lubricate either of these drills with water.

Drilling with larger cylindrical drills is called *core drilling* because the primary purpose is to produce a usable core of material. There are also many instances in which the void is the objective and the core a by-product. Such drills are used for cutting out solid circular bracelets and rings, usually of jade (3-21); for cutting blanks or preforms for round stones; for opening apertures in carvings; for removing material from the interior of vessels and other hollow objects; and for cutting out preforms for beads and other cylindrical forms (3-22).

Sintered-diamond core drills—drills in which diamond grit is impregnated throughout the wall of the drill—are the most efficient and the most expensive. Drilling should be done underwater for maximum efficiency. Although other lubricants can be used, water flushes out the cut best. These larger drills should be operated in a regular machinist's or woodworker's drill press, but portable hand drills mounted in suitable presses can be used if the chuck capacity is large enough. Most of these manufactured drills are fitted onto a 1 1/2" shank.

To prepare the machine for drilling, a metal pan is fastened securely to the table of the drill press. The piece to be drilled is attached to the bottom of the pan with dop wax and covered with water (3-23). The drill must be raised from time to time to allow water to run into the cut. It is best not to cement down the core area: this allows the core to remain in the drill when it is cut free and the vacant hole to show when you raise the drill. If the core is stuck to the pan, it is sometimes difficult to tell when the drill has cut through. The drilling procedure is the same for home-made diamond-charged drills.

With uncharged bare metal core drills a slurry of silicon-carbide grit is used instead of the plain-water bath. To cut down on the amount of grit required, a small container is set up around the hole to be drilled. It can be built of modeling clay, or a section of metal tubing in the appropriate size can be cemented down with dopping wax, paraffin, or any other material that will seal the joint. The mixture of grit and water is poured into the container to just cover the work. The slurry should be a soupy mix that flows freely. Grit sizes can range from 120 to 220: finer grains produce smoother cuts. The drill is operated in the same manner as for diamond-charged drills, with intermittent raising to allow the mixture to run into the hole. For deep holes fresh grit may have to be added from time to time as the grains become worn. The drilling speed is much slower than with diamond drills. Whereas 1/4″-deep holes can be drilled in jade in 5 or 6 minutes with the former, as much as 30 minutes may be needed with the grit-and-bare-drill method. With both types of drills the core remaining in the drill can be removed by pushing it out from the inside with a rod. A hole is provided for this purpose in the top end of bare metal drills. Diamond drills may have a spring pin inside the drill. Some of these also have a water connection through a hose: water pressure extrudes the core when the drill cuts through. This is helpful for industrial uses in which provisions for water disposal are provided, but this kind of setup is usually inconvenient for the individual craftsman.

3-22.

3-21.

3-23.

63

4. Special Techniques

For want of a better term more advanced, specialized techniques not discussed in the preceding chapter are classed here as special techniques. For the most part the same principles are involved, and much of the same equipment is used. If you have thoroughly mastered the basic techniques, you will find no insurmountable difficulties in more advanced work. Special techniques are: tumbling, faceting, spheres and beads, hollow forms, inlay, intarsia, parquetry, marquetry, mosaic, carving, engraving, encrusting, etching, and hand cutting.

Tumbling

Tumbling is an automatic rather than a hand technique. It is extremely popular, because the equipment and materials are comparatively inexpensive, and the results rather astonishing. Rough materials can be broken to required sizes, placed in the simple machine, and taken out as highly polished gemstones of irregular shape. They can be mounted by gluing bell caps onto the surface and attaching jewelry findings (earring and cuff-link backs, bracelet links, chains) to form complete pieces of jewelry.

At first glance tumbled stones, or *baroques*, as they are usually called, are quite intriguing in shape, seeming to resemble waterworn pebbles found in stream beds. But close examination reveals that the shapes that at first appeared unique are actually repeated again and again, due to the uniform mechanical breakage of the rough materials, and soon become tiresome. In viewing rows of bins in the hobby shops, filled with every possible variety of tumbled stones, one's feeling for the beauty and attraction of gem materials is somehow dulled and repelled. The prices, quoted by the pound, are startlingly cheap, because the tumbling process is almost completely automatic. Novelty and hobby shops, even the corner drugstore, offer kits of baroques, bell caps, findings, and epoxy cement—all that is needed to produce instant jewelry. The market is so flooded with these mass-produced stones and glued-up jewelry that one's respect for beautiful gem materials is unconsciously lessened. The overabundance and misuse have an inevitable cheapening effect. Popularization and commercialization have also tended to stifle the latent creativity of many people who become interested in gemstones by making it possible to produce tumbled gems and tasteless jewelry with little effort of the mind or hand. People are diverted into an activity that is neither an art nor a craft but a commercial substitute for creativity and fine craftsmanship.

Why is tumbling included in this book? Because the fault lies in the abuse and misuse of the process, not in the process itself. There is nothing wrong with automatic equipment as long as it furthers a creative end result. The slabbing saw and the vibrating lap are examples of automatic machines that can accomplish preliminary stages of creatively designed objects. The tumbler can be used legitimately and effectively in the same way.

Simple shapes and small slabs can be preformed by sawing or grinding, then sanding and polishing in the tumbler. Sharp edges and corners always become at least slightly rounded in tumbling, which is no great disadvantage in the case of slabs: the edges can be ground square and refinished by regular sanding and polishing if desired. With experience it is possible to calculate and allow for the degree of alteration in preparing the preforms (4-1).

Another practical use of tumbling is in testing rough material that occurs as small pebbles. It is often difficult or impossible to judge the quality of such mate-

4-1. Necklace, preformed tumbled strips of different-colored jade, gold tubing.

rial in its natural state: imperfections and fractures may not show up until the piece is polished. These stones can be ground to remove the rough exterior and semipolished in the tumbler, which will reveal which pieces can be cut into gems without a great deal of handwork, a timesaving practice indeed!

In the tumbling process the drum is filled to just over half its capacity with stones and coarse silicon-carbide grit, and water is added to just cover the stones. The motor is turned on, and the drum rotates continuously until the coarse-grinding stage is complete. Then the stones are removed and rinsed until every trace of grit is removed, and the drum is also washed perfectly clean. It is then reloaded with the same stones and a charge of fine grit, and the fine-grinding stage is completed in the same manner, which leaves the stones with a soft semipolish. Everything is cleaned as before, and the stones are polished by adding the appropriate polishing compound for the particular material. Plastic pellets or bits of leather scrap are often added to assist the process. This step results in a fairly good polish, which can be improved by a final step of tumbling in a detergent solution. The complete process requires days or weeks, depending on the type of material and the efficiency of the tumbler. For further information consult the bibliography.

Faceting

Faceting is another mechanical process, although it is not yet completely automated. No creative ability is required by the faceter: setting and maintaining the proper angles for producing any standard cut are purely a matter of following directions. The only skill involved is in judging the depth to which each facet should be cut in order to produce an identical row, and even this element is automatically controlled in some machines. Hand faceting will eventually become completely mechanized, at least for commercial purposes, and the technique itself is not artistically creative: no machine will ever be able to automatically produce an aesthetically significant result; it can only do a more perfect mechanical job than the human hand. One has to admire the skill of faceters who use the older jamb-peg, or backrest, assembly. With the jamb-peg setup the angles of the facets are set by eye, and precise judgment and touch, resulting from experience, are demanded. But the aim of both hand and machine faceting is to produce mechanically perfect stones by following the charts available for all standard cuts. These cuts were developed slowly by trial and error and the science of optics during the rather long history of the faceting technique. Any deviation from the prescribed relative angles of the main facets in these cuts will almost inevitably result in less brilliant stones, especially in the transparent materials usually faceted. New cuts are developed from time to time, mostly by amateur faceters, and the geometric possibilities are seemingly endless, yet the constant optical properties of each material remain the determining factor if maximum brilliance and color are to be achieved. This restriction applies to the relative angles of the facets, not to their pattern, but there is hardly enough freedom within the geometry of what is still conventional faceting to allow much opportunity for truly creative expression. Only by rejecting the principal objective of faceting, to display the greatest possible brilliance and color in every stone, is aesthetic innovation possible.

Faceting can be approached from a different viewpoint—to cut arbitrary facets or asymmetrical patterns in order to create uniquely shaped stones for particular applications. For instance, facets and rounded areas can be combined in a single stone to create surface contrast. A designer may well be more interested in creating a unique shape to fit a jewelry design than in exploiting the brilliance of the material: he may not want the flash and glitter that a standard cut offers but rather an entirely different and original effect. A few strategically placed facets can enable gleams of light to penetrate the mysterious depths of deeply colored stones such as amethyst, ruby, and garnet; facets can also be cut on opaque and translucent materials that are not customarily faceted. Some of these materials have special qualities: for example, hematite, the pure, opaque, black iron ore, can be faceted to reflect a brilliant display of light from flat surfaces polished to mirrorlike perfection.

Faceting offers many possibilities to craftsmen searching for personal, creative means of expression. A good way to explore the technique is to cut facets freehand on inexpensive material, using the standard grinding wheel (4-2). A backrest assembly is the ideal instrument. Try combining faceted, rounded, and concave surfaces. The latter are not difficult to do with small grinding, sanding, and polishing wheels and a carving machine; facets and rounded areas require only the regular grinders and sanders. Quartz materials—amethyst, citrine, clear quartz, quartz with golden rutile inclusions—are the easiest to experiment with, since they do not require special polishing laps and methods, as do harder stones.

To grind facets on the circular face, the wheel must be kept perfectly smooth by frequent dressing—180 or 220 grit is suggested for most materials. The facets are cut by moving the stone upward in as close to a vertical plane as possible. Properly done, this will produce facets that appear flat except to minute inspection. For perfectly flat planes try a final step of truing them up on the flat side of the wheel. It is difficult to set the stone down flat every time, but it can be done with practice.

4-2.

Sanding is also done by moving the stone in a vertical plane, taking care not to round the adjoining edges of the facets. A soft-backed wheel cannot be used: cork is the best backing material for this purpose. A belt sander with the back plate in place is preferable to the drum type, and a disk sander can also be used if it has a proper firm backing. Polish quartz, particularly the flat facets, with a hard leather wheel and either tin or chromium-oxide polishing compound. This should produce a brilliant surface on material sanded with 120, 220, and 320 cloth.

Both freehand faceting and a more advanced technique, in which the optical effects of the material are calculated and exploited in an unconventional manner, offer great possibilities for investigation and development, particularly in relation to creative jewelry design.

Beads and Spheres
Bead and sphere making is another mechanical process that many amateurs find fascinating. Spheres are usually used only for display, while beads are most often strung to form necklaces. Neither are creative objects in themselves, but they can be used occasionally as elements in a creative design.

The process is essentially the same for the preform stage, whether the ball is small or large. A geometrically accurate cube is sawed out; the corners are sawed or ground off to form flat faces; and the cube is gradually reduced in this way to form an eighteen-sided polygon with all corresponding faces as nearly equal as possible. The preform is ground either by hand or mechanically into a true sphere, then sanded and polished. Small balls or beads (up to 3/4") can be made by using holders of wood, bamboo, or metal tubing. The end of the tube is beveled inward at a 45° angle and the ball, larger than the diameter of the holder, rests in the end as in a cup. On a rest set slightly below the center of the grinding wheel, the tube is steadied, and the ball brought up against the face of the running wheel. By moving the holder from side to side on the rest and manipulating the ball with the fingertips, it can be made to spin in all directions, gradually grinding it to a near-perfect sphere. It is finished in the same way on sanding and polishing wheels. Balls that are too small to be manipulated in the tube holder can be made with a wooden dowel rod, in the end of which a shallow cuplike depression is ground with a steel burr. The depression should be at least twice the diameter of the ball in width and no less than half the diameter in depth. Grinding is done as with the tube holder, but fingertip control is not possible. The trick is to apply very light pressure to hold it in the cup—

too much and it will jump out. Both grinding and sanding are done at fairly slow speed. You can polish the ball on a hard felt wheel, but cementing a thin piece of felt in the depression and saturating it with polishing compound will assist the process.

4-3. Eskimo jade-and-ivory bead necklace, made by George Cleveland.

cross section of tube and solid-rod holders

4-4.

If many balls or beads are required, it is more practical to buy them from a dealer or make them in a bead mill. Follow the simple instructions that manufacturers provide with their machines.

Larger balls, usually called spheres, must be ground by a different method, although the preform is essentially the same as for the smaller balls. It can be formed very accurately by following these steps: first saw as perfect a cube as possible; inscribe a perfect circle with a permanent marker on one face; saw off the four square edges, using the circle as a guide; saw off the remaining original square edges. This will yield the eighteen-sided preform. To make the cuts accurately, use a wooden jig block with a V-cut at right angles to its base. Mark

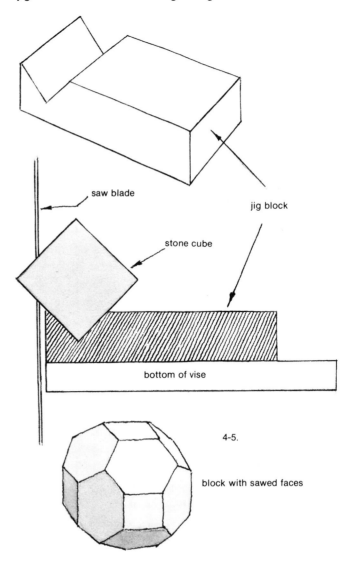

saw blade

jig block

stone cube

bottom of vise

4-5.

block with sawed faces

67

the position of the jig in the vise, because it must remain in this position until all the cuts are made; the preform is simply turned in the vee for each cut. Only the first four cuts are at right angles to the face of the preform; all others are at a slant, which means that they must be started very slowly to prevent the blade from slipping out of line on the slanting surface.

Rough grinding to eliminate the angles where planes meet must be done by hand. First mark each face with a permanent center dot. It acts as a guide to preserve the diameter while grinding, which should be done by turning the preform against the wheel on a steady rest set in front of the grinder. The next step is smooth grinding with a pair of cutters made from short sections of iron pipe, with one end of each ground to a 45° angle inward. One cutter has a fitting that allows it to be mounted on the shaft of either a horizontal or vertical arbor. The wall of the cutters is fairly thick to allow sufficient grinding surface, and their diameter should be 1/3 to 3/4 that of the sphere. A thick paste of coarse abrasive is dabbed on the cutters and the sphere. The free cutter is held in the hand against the ball in the fixed cutter, with the machine running at no more than 500 r.p.m. Keep working the hand-held cutter over the surface and replenish the grit occasionally. Turn the sphere intermittently by hand so that the entire surface is reached.

As it becomes more perfect, it will start to spin on the cutters and the work will speed up. Continue through a series of finer grits until a good prepolish is achieved. Polishing is comparatively easy with most materials. Spheres more than 2″ in diameter should be polished on a steady rest as in grinding, but smaller balls can be polished freehand or fastened to a heavy dop stick.

Sphere-making machines that work automatically are commercially available, but it is unlikely that the creative lapidary will do enough work of this kind to justify the expense.

Hollow Forms
Hollow forms include all kinds of vessels and containers from plates and saucers through cups, bowls, urns, bottles, vases, compotes, incense burners, jars, and boxes. The Chinese were particularly proficient and versatile in this field—their magnificent work tends to fill modern craftsmen with despair rather than inspiration. Still there is always room for the development of contemporary styles and concepts, and it is technically a good deal easier and faster to form a hollow vessel in stone with modern equipment. Many of the tools and techniques developed by the Chinese can be used in modern work—indeed, most of the procedures cannot be accomplished by any other means. Techniques vary

4-6.

4-7.

68

somewhat depending on the shape and the material. Nephrite jade is the ideal material for hollow forms because of its resistance to fracture both in working and in use as a finished piece, but many other materials can be used, such as agate, jasper, rock crystal, or alabaster. The foremost requirement is that the material be free of flaws and fractures. You cannot examine it too carefully before starting work—it is extremely disconcerting to expend great effort on a piece only to discover a hidden flaw that renders it useless for the purpose intended.

There are several ways of removing material to form the inner void: which method to use usually depends on the type of material that is available and on the shape of the piece. For a bowl with an approximately hemispherical or shallower void the traditional Chinese method is to make multiple parallel cuts into the material from above with a circular saw. This requires a saw with an arbor that can be raised and lowered, a feature of the foot-powered Chinese saw. The only modern saws with this feature are those in which the blade is on an overarm assembly and cuts by being lowered manually onto the work. The cuts are shallower near the edge of the bowl and become consecutively deeper as they approach the center. The surface is crossed in one direction, then the piece is turned and similar cuts are made at right angles to the first. The standing square posts left by the cuts are easily broken off by wedging with a screwdriver or similar tapered tool (4-8). Toward the center the posts may measure up to 3/8" in thickness, allowing you to save some usable material.

Another traditional hollowing implement is the core drill. It is most appropriate for vessels with straight or steep sides. To operate the drill, a standard drill press is required. The block of material is secured to the table of the press and centered under the drill. A comparatively small-diameter drill is used for the center hole; increasingly larger drills, for the concentric cuts (4-9). Water must always cover the work. The first core is broken off with a chisel and hammer by striking a sharp diagonal blow against its upper end. A small-diameter diamond-charged saw is used to cut loose the wall of the next hollow cylindrical core. The saw must have a long enough shank to reach the bottom of the hole. It can be operated on a hand-held rotary machine such as a portable electric hand drill. You will have to make the saw yourself in order to obtain the long shank; the most practical blade is the notched diamond-charged disk described in chapter 2. The remaining cylinders are cut loose in the same manner. As the center opening increases in size with removal of successive cores, larger-diameter blades can be used for greater efficiency. Un-

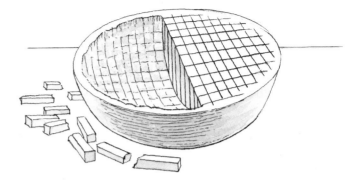

4-8.

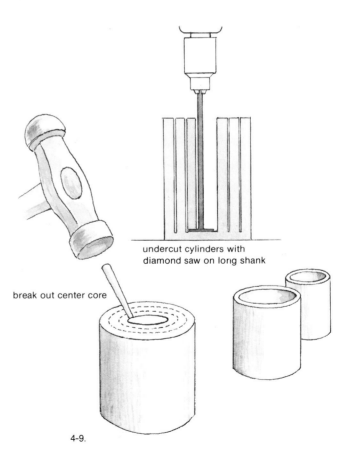

undercut cylinders with diamond saw on long shank

break out center core

4-9.

broken cylinders can be used for other projects such as boxes and jars, which can be fitted with separate bottom disks. If you decide not to preserve the cylinders, they can be broken out by wedging.

Either of the two hollowing methods will leave the bottom surface of the void very rough and uneven. Grinding away the irregularities and smoothing the surface for the final polish can be done in several ways, depending on the size and shape of the piece. If it is light-weight and small enough to be manipulated easily by hand, a fixed arbor can be used to hold the grinding tool. If it is too bulky and heavy for hand-control, the grinder must be on a freely movable machine. In the first case either the drill press or a fixed carving-machine arbor will serve; in the second a flexible shaft, portable hand drill, or small grinder designed for offhand use is appropriate. Small grinding wheels 3″ or 4″ in diameter, large mounted ball-shaped grinders, or similarly shaped soft iron tools with silicon-carbide grits can all be used to finish the opening. To sand the interior curved surface, use soft wooden wheels, which can be contoured for a suitable curve. For polishing use felt wheels, leather wheels, or muslin buffs to suit the material.

The rough hollowing should be done before shaping the exterior, because there is less likelihood of cracking the wall when the fins or posts left by the saw or core drill are broken off if the piece is left in the block. Remove waste material from the outside carefully to preserve the proper thickness of the wall. Large pieces can be clamped at various angles in the slabbing saw to remove excess material. Judgment and ingenuity in sawing can save a lot of time at the grinder. Grinding the rough exterior to a true contour also requires some ingenuity. The larger the vessel, the greater the difficulty in turning the piece against the grinding wheel on a stationary arbor. If the piece is too large to be manipulated easily by hand, a portable, hand-held machine must be used.

Several machines have been devised that hollow and grind the interior automatically. One uses the exterior of one bowl to grind the interior of another, with silicon-carbide-grit slurry furnishing the abrasive action. The same principle can be used to operate a machine with a grinding wheel as the grinding head rather than another piece of gem material (4-10). Such equipment is not commercially available, but you might find it worthwhile to build your own if you do a lot of hollowing.

These machines waste a considerable amount of material, which can increase the cost a great deal if it is valuable. To overcome this situation, it is possible to build a machine that salvages the interior of a hemispherical vessel intact (4-11). A hemispherical cutter in the form of a thin metal cup charged with diamond grit is rotated by a motor, with a chuck holding the shank of the tool. The piece is centered and attached to a tailstock, which is hinged to rotate 180° around an axis that intersects the center of the cup vertically. The piece can be rotated on the tail stock by hand. The cup, which must be lubricated with a water drip, starts cutting at one edge of the blank, while the piece is gradually turned on both vertical and horizontal axes simultaneously by hand. The horizontal rotation moves the cutter around the rim; the vertical rotation allows the cup to cut deeper toward the center. The cutting action is continued until the entire interior is released, except for a small-diameter post at the center. This post is easily snapped off, and the hemisphere detached. The small irregularity left in the center is easily ground level with the rest of the interior. The cutter cup can be made either by spinning a sheet of metal over a wooden form in a spinning lathe or by raising it from sheet metal with silversmith's hammers. Copper 24-gauge sheet is suggested. The edge is charged with diamond grit as for saws and core drills (see chapter 2). Inside and outside surfaces should also be scored and charged to assist the cutting and to prevent binding against any irregularities produced in the formation of the cutter cup. This method allows the smooth void left by the cutter to be used as the interior of a bowl. The exterior is formed by removing excess material with multiple saw cuts and grinding to proper contour. The solid hemisphere that is removed from the inside can be used for a second bowl of slightly smaller size, which can be hollowed out by the same procedure.

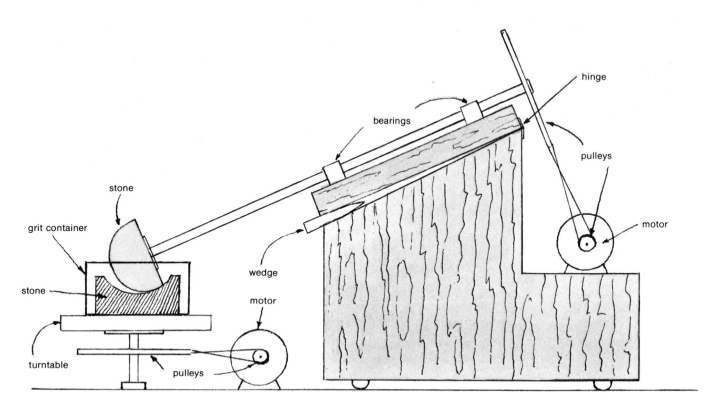

4-10.

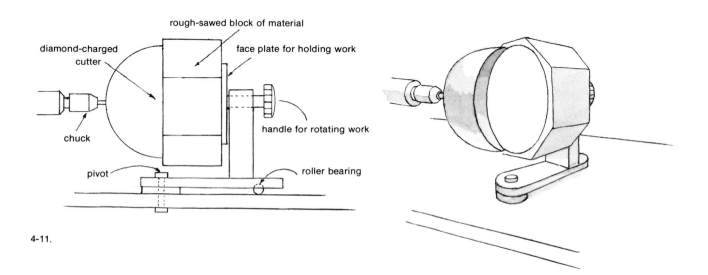

4-11.

Vessels with openings that are smaller in diameter than the interior pose a different problem: a central core must be drilled and broken out to form a hollow shaft in the center through which tools can be inserted to enlarge the interior. Any opening that is not extremely small will allow a tool to be angled to reach a wider area than the opening itself (4-12), but a curved tool, which can be inserted at an angle, then straightened in the hole to press against the side, is required if the opening is very small. The Chinese used flexible wires for this purpose (4-13). Such tools are made of soft iron and used with silicon-carbide grit and water. They wear out rapidly, and grinding is slow, for a lot of material must be removed and the tools are not very efficient. A simple and more effective tool utilizes a hinge pin and a rubber band (4-14). This principle can be utilized to hollow out even fairly large vessels with narrow openings. Several different-contoured grinders must be used as the work progresses. Objects with narrow openings should have fairly thin walls to reduce the weight and to create a graceful rather than a clumsy effect. Translucent materials in particular should have thin walls to allow transmitted light to pass through, and the walls must be polished inside as well as out.

Inlay

Inlay refers to the embedding of one piece in another. The materials involved can be the same, such as stone into stone, or different, such as stone into metal or metal into stone. With the former it is easy to secure the inlay permanently with an epoxy cement, since stone surfaces bond reliably to each other with this type of adhesive. With the latter the bond may release from the metal but not from the stone. Although there is little chance that a metal inlay will detach and fall out, it is best to take the precaution of cutting recesses in the metal on the surface that contacts the stone to allow the epoxy to key itself into these notches and hold the metal in place (4-15).

Inlaying a design into an unbroken field is the most difficult type. The design is drawn on paper, and the outline is transferred to the background material. If the background is stone, the recess, or *bed*, to hold the design must be routed out to the proper depth with rotary grinding wheels and points. The bed must be cut deep enough to hold the inlaid piece securely, and the inlay must be thick enough not to be cracked or broken in use. The walls of the bed should be sloped very slightly toward the center. It is fairly easy to cut straight or

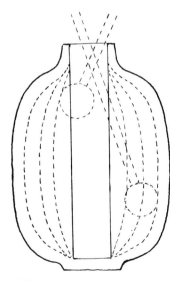

4-12.

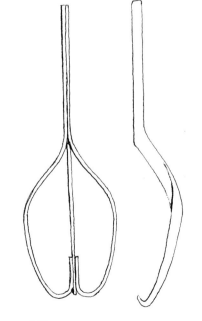

rubber band

hinge pin

cross section of vessel

4-13.

4-14.

curved contours, but angles are more difficult. Since the rotary tools are circular in shape, an angle cannot be cut without leaving a shallow curved wall in the corner. Grinding it down to an acceptable depth so that a fragile point will not be left on the inlay piece usually requires handwork with a flat metal tool and silicon-carbide grit (4-16). The bed should be ground down to a fairly even surface, but it does not have to be perfectly smooth. It is not always necessary to cut a bed: an opening can be cut through the background piece to receive the inlay, and a backing of metal or even of another piece of stone can be applied. It is easier to cut the angles and curves for the inlay with this method.

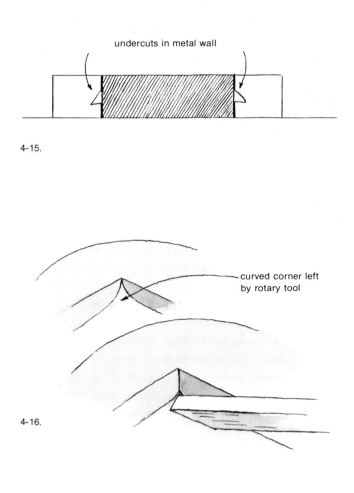

undercuts in metal wall

4-15.

curved corner left
by rotary tool

4-16.

To cut the inlay accurately, you need an exact outline of the recess. Do not use the same pattern that was used to lay out the recess: there is always some variation between that outline and the outline of the recess itself. One method of obtaining an accurate transfer is to paste or tape a piece of medium-weight paper in position over the recess and, using the side rather than the point of a hard lead pencil, to carefully rub the outline of the recess. The rubbing that results will have a sharp black line in the center, marking the sharp edges of the recess. Take the paper off the stone and cut out the pattern along the black line with a sharp knife point. Paste the pattern face up on the inlay material and ink in the exposed area around the pattern with a waterproof marker. When the paper is removed, a stenciled image of the pattern will be left on the stone. Make trimming cuts with the trim saw as close as possible to the outline, then grind away the remaining excess material, leaving a tiny margin around the design until you make sure that it fits in the recess. Keep testing and grinding until the fit is perfect. Inlays are usually flush with the surrounding surface, but they can project in relief above the surface: there can even be several levels in the finished design. If the finished surface is to be level, the inlay should initially project slightly above the background, and the surface of the entire piece lapped carefully until it is smooth, sanded, and polished. The grinding should be minimal, since the inlay may be relatively thin, and the joints between the pieces not as perfect underneath as at the point of contact. For inlays designed to project above the background the pieces should be finished before they are assembled. The epoxy with which the inlay is cemented in place can be colored with dry pigment to match the color of the background. This will also tend to make any slight imperfections in the fitting unnoticeable, but a perfect fit should be your goal.

Techniques of securing metal-and-stone inlays vary with the metal and the character of the design. If the metal is relatively inexpensive—brass or copper, for instance—the piece may be fairly thick, and the technique described above for stone inlays can be used. The only difference is that the edges of the metal should have a few recesses, or undercuts. If the metal is too thin for undercuts to be made in the edges, posts should be soldered to the back at strategic points, drilling the background and inserting the posts as the inlay is embedded. If they pass completely through the backing, they can be peened over to hold securely; if not, they should be notched so that the epoxy will hold, as with the heavy-plate edges mentioned above.

4-17. Navajo bola tie, silver inlay in ironwood, made by Kenny Begay.

If the inlay is linear, a different technique, often called *encrusting* or *encrustation*, can be used. The edges of the lines are cut in at an angle on each side so that the groove is slightly larger at the bottom, and a soft metal wire is inlaid into this groove (4-19). It can be tapped carefully into place, then forced down into the cut with a burnisher and heavy pressure. The soft metal will expand into the undercuts and be anchored permanently. The surface is then sanded level and polished. Fine silver and 24K gold are used for linear designs because of their malleability; 22K gold can be used, but it must be fully annealed. Jade is the best background material because it will not chip with tapping or pressure.

Commercial encrusting, used to engrave initials, signets, monograms, or insignias on the surface of ring stones, is done in a different manner. The lines are engraved and gold leaf is applied to the design. A thin, rapid-drying varnish is painted in the cuts, and the gold leaf is laid on the varnished surface while it is wet with a soft brush. The leaf adheres to the varnish permanently. After the varnish has dried, the excess leaf is trimmed away, leaving the engraved design in gold. Since all the lines are cut below the surface, the gold leaf receives no wear and remains in place very satisfactorily.

4-18. Wedding rings, black jade, 14K-yellow-gold cast inlay.

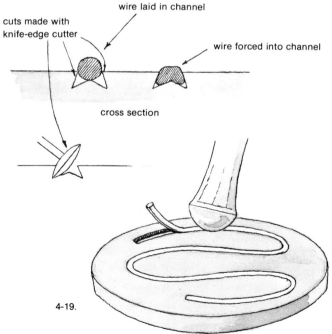

4-19.

Inlay of metal into stone and stone into metal can also be accomplished by casting the metal, either as the background or the inlay, with the stone in place. Some designs can be executed only with this technique, but many factors must be taken into consideration, and the results are often disappointing. The reaction of the materials to high burnout temperatures and to sudden contact with molten metal are particularly important, and even at best, results are hard to predict with certainty. This technique requires patience, experimentation, and systematic recording of results in order to develop its unique possibilities, as well as a knowledge of the standard procedures of lost-wax casting of metals.

As a general rule stones 8 or above in hardness can be cast in place successfully by placing them in the wax pattern and investing in the usual manner, but certain precautions must be taken. Although the stones usually do not alter in color or clarity and are not cracked by the burnout heat or the contact with molten metal, the setting must be designed to avoid exerting damaging pressure as it shrinks in cooling. Acute edges and thin sections may be chipped or cracked by the shrinking metal if this stress is not taken into account. Calculation of the stress must include the characteristics of the material: if it is brittle or has weak cleavage planes, more caution must be observed than if it is tough and resistant to fracture.

Attempts have been made to cast materials below 8 in hardness with some success. Some are ruined by minimal heat and pressure, but others can be cast if the proper procedure is followed. In general the lowest possible burnout temperature should be used, and burnout time held to an absolute minimum. Most waxes will not burn out thoroughly at temperatures less than 1,200° F., but Slaycris wax, obtainable from dental-supply houses, burns out cleanly at 800°. Unfortunately it is rather expensive, but it is not only ideal in terms of burnout temperature but also for carving, building, and texturing, since it has no "memory" and is not fragile.

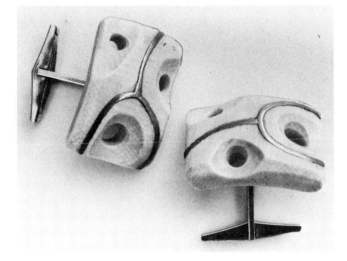

4-20. Cuff links, mammoth ivory, 24K-gold inlay.

4-21. Bracelet, black jade, 24K-gold inlay.

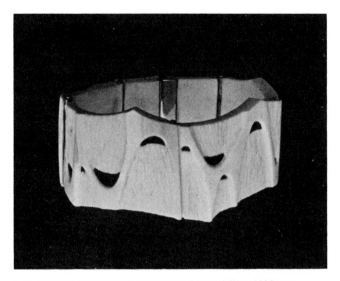

4-22. Bracelet, walrus ivory, caribou-hoof inlay, 14K-gold hinges.

It comes in only one form, a small, flat can containing about 2 ounces. Sprue wires must be constructed or extruded from a wax wire-making machine. The following procedure is recommended. Preheat the furnace to 800°, place the flask in the furnace with the sprue hole up, hold the temperature until no discoloration shows, and cast with as little time lapse as possible between removal from the furnace and injection of the metal. Burnout time can be 1 hour or less for small flasks. The flask should be cooled down as rapidly as possible without completely immersing it in water. Set the flask on the sprue-hole end in about 1″ of water. Leave it in place until it is cool enough to handle, then dig out the casting with a knife blade.

The casting-inlay technique varies depending on whether stone is inlaid into metal, or metal into stone. Metal-into-stone inlays are the easier type. The recess for the metal is carved in the gem material and filled with wax, and sprues are attached. The inlay should be keyed in place by making undercuts in the wall of the seat. This type of inlay can be as elaborate as desired if sprues are provided to carry the metal to all areas (4-23). Stone-into-metal inlays are more complicated because of the metal-shrinkage factor: only a few stones are strong enough to withstand the pressure of being completely surrounded by a field of solid metal. Both nephrite and jadeite are suitable, and some other gemstones will work out successfully if the surrounding metal is light enough. The Slaycris wax discussed above makes it possible to cast in place some gem materials that are ruined by normal burnout temperatures. The following materials under 8 in hardness were tested by the author and found to suffer no changes when kept at 800° for 1 hour: jasper, agate, jadeite, nephrite (black, white, pale green, deep green), lapis lazuli, sodalite, moonstone, peristerite, labradorite, sunstone (India), peridot, tourmaline, pyrope garnet, and citrine. Nephrite jade showed variable reactions: some of the more translucent material began to show opacity with some alteration of color. Turquoise, chrysocolla, malachite, variscite—the copper derivatives—are ruined by comparatively low heat; amethyst and amazonite lose color; golden tigereye becomes reddish.

You should run your own tests, since different specimens may react differently. Small samples can be tested by holding them in the furnace at 800° for the maximum expected burnout time. Tests should also be run to determine the amount of time required—Slaycris wax burns out more rapidly than other casting waxes. Burnout-temperature testing does not provide utlimate proof that a given material will react favorably under all con-ditions because it ignores the possible effect of the molten metal at a much higher temperature when it contacts the stone. Some stones are more adversely affected by this contact than others and require that the contact area be kept at a minimum. These requirements must be determined by experience, since individual situations vary too widely to be covered.

Stone-into-metal and metal-into-stone inlays can be accomplished without the uncertainties of the above method by casting the metal part separately. The stone is first cut to the required shape; if it is to act as a background, the recess for the inlay is carved out and filled with wax just as if it were to be cast in place. The wax is carefully removed, sprued, and cast by itself; then the sprues are cut off, and it is fitted into the recess. It can be held in place with an epoxy cement if the edges are undercut as described above. To prevent stones from sticking to the wax, coat them with a mixture of glycerine and a drop or two of alcohol.

4-23.

Many craftsmen have difficulty in fitting the pieces together without additional work on the stone or seat after the casting has been made. The casting must be done precisely to avoid shrinkage of the interior of the mold. An investment formulated to minimize shrinkage must be used. What is generally termed shrinkage is actually expansion: the void shrinks and becomes smaller because of the expansion of the investment. This can be

4-24. Bracelet, flexible links of grass-green jade, 14K-gold clasp.

4-25. Pendant, black jade, 14K-gold inlay cast by lost-wax process and refitted in carved recesses.

avoided by lining the inside of the casting flask with a layer or two of wet asbestos. This allows the investment to expand outward as well as inward, which is impossible in a bare metal flask. Since very little expansion is involved (less than 1% with a dental investment) and it is cut in half by this procedure, fitting difficulties will rarely arise. Metal shrinkage must also be avoided with stone-into-metal inlays, because the seat tends to become too small for the stone. Casting at as low a temperature as is practical and cooling as fast as possible by immersion will keep shrinkage at a minimum. These precautions are unnecessary in most cases for metal-into-stone inlays.

If the inlay is flush with the background, it is best to do the final leveling and polishing after the pieces are embedded to assure an even surface, with one exception: if the different materials cannot be polished with the same polishing agent. In this case they must be polished separately and carefully embedded at the same level.

Intarsia, Parquetry, and Marquetry
These inlay derivatives are slightly different from true inlay and from each other (see the section on pictorial compositions in chapter 5), but the same techniques are generally used. Pieces of similar materials are fitted against each other rather than being embedded, as in true inlay. A full-scale reference design is drawn on paper, and a tracing is made—a pattern that shows the outline of each separate piece—on water-resistant material, then fastened flat on a smooth, level surface. A second identical pattern is made and cut along the outline into separate pieces, which are cemented to the respective slabs that are to be cut and ground to fit each other. If the paper is not highly resistant to water, it can be coated with shellac or lacquer after it has been applied. As the pieces are ground to the outline, they are fitted onto the first pattern piece by piece like a jigsaw puzzle until the design is complete and all the joints fit as perfectly as possible. A third pattern exactly like the first two but *in reverse* is then made. It can be traced on transparent tissue so that the design is visible in reverse. It is secured on a flat, level backing, and the pieces are assembled on it face down and cemented together with epoxy. After the cement has set thoroughly, the paper is removed, the excess epoxy scraped away from the front, and the assemblage finished as a wall hanging, box top, tabletop, or any similar project.

Many parts of the outline can be cut accurately with the trim saw and trimmed as close to the final outline as possible, but most of the final shaping is done on the grinder. All except very small pieces with intricate contours can be ground on a regular 6" or 8" wheel; for the latter you may have to resort to a very small wheel operated on the carving machine. For the large grinder a 220-grit or finer wheel, dressed smooth at all times, should be used. Set a steady rest in front of the wheel, level with its exact center. The edge of the slab, ground while it lies flat on the rest, will have only a slight curve from top to bottom in cross section, which will leave only a very tiny gap between the pieces on the bottom side when they are fitted together. This has some mechanical advantage, since a thick epoxy joint is stronger than a very thin one (5–48). It is helpful to dress one edge of the grinder to a very small radius and the other to a larger one to grind curves with different contours.

Mosaic

Stone material can be utilized in a similar manner to standard colored-glass mosaic. This technique uses small, flat fragments, called *tesserae*, which are set in a cement grout. No effort is made to fit the pieces tightly against each other without showing a joint, as in the traditional mosaic: instead, the perceptible joints are used as an effect in the design. Stone mosaic is rather rare because most gem materials cannot be broken easily and accurately with nippers, as can standard mosaic materials, and common, inexpensive gem materials do not have the brilliant colors available in glass tesserae. The mosaicist would tend to think of gem materials as a poor substitute for the glass that he is accustomed to use, yet there are undoubtedly many creative possibilities in using the technique in a modified, arbitrary way. For instance, the pieces need not be approximately the same size and shape, as in regular mosaic work: contrasts between individual pieces can create an interesting pattern or composition. The cement joints can also provide an interesting background pattern.

Carving

Stones of almost any material and of any size, from the tiniest gems used for jewelry to small freestanding sculptures, can be carved. Some materials are preferable to others: in general compact stones without weak cleavage planes are the most desirable; brittle and excessively soft materials are best avoided altogether. The following carving techniques can be applied to most suitable materials. Specific materials and techniques are discussed later in this chapter. There are two main categories of carving: *relief and in-the-round*. In some respects the latter is more demanding, because it is more difficult to visualize a design in three dimensions than in two.

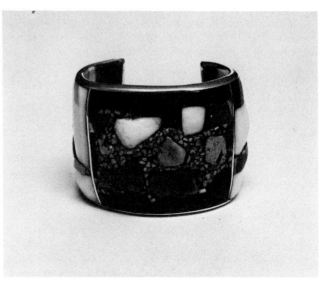

4-26. Zuni silver bracelet, coral, shell, jet, turquoise mosaic inlay, made by Roger Tsabetsaye.

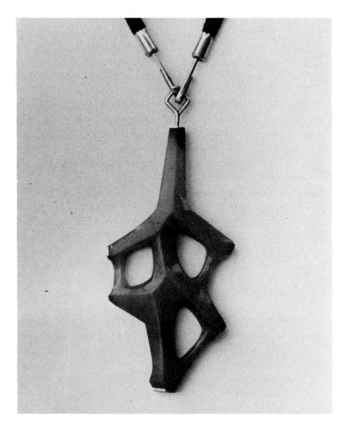

4-27. Pendant, carved jade, 14K gold.

78

The three-dimensional aspect of the form must be carried out fully, and the finished object consistent and effective from all sides. On the other hand, a high degree of technical and artistic ability is also required to produce relief carvings, pictorial forms and surfaces that create the *illusion* of depth and distance.

4-28. Eskimo seal-shaped pin, carved jade, made by Peter Seeganna.

4-29. Bracelet, carved green jade, 14K gold, spring-tempered band.

Relief Carving

Relief carving is also of two general types: *high-relief* and *low-relief*, or *bas-relief*. In the first projections above the background plane may rise more than half the diameter of the form represented. Occasionally some forms may be carved in-the-round and partially detached from the background. In the second type the modulations of surface planes barely rise above the surrounding background. Depth is created by illusion, and the effect is more pictorial than sculptural. Both kinds of relief carving are essentially the same in technique: the work is executed almost entirely with rotary points and wheels (see chapter 2). Guidelines for the design are drawn on the surface of the material with a waterproof marking pen and incised with a small knife-edge diamond or silicon-carbide wheel. Full-depth background areas are removed with broader-faced grinding tools, leaving the higher areas in relief. Intermediate planes are leveled to their respective depths until a rough approximation of the design is achieved. Rough forms are then modulated, and the details are worked out and finished.

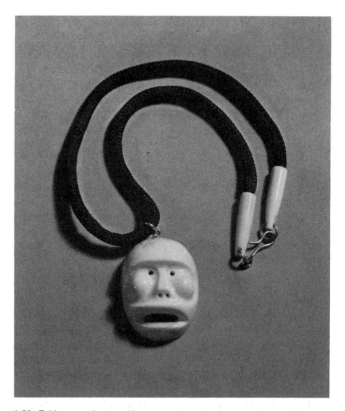

4-30. Eskimo pendant necklace, carved walrus-ivory mask, made by Victor Swan.

If you know how to use the equipment, relief is simply a matter of applying the carving technique to a flat, continuous surface. It is harder to control the depth of cut on a flat plane than in-the-round, particularly if a perfectly flat background is required. The boundaries of figures rising above the background are not incised below the surface in the classical bas-relief: the forms should appear as if they were lying flat against it, creating an illusion of space behind the figure when viewed at the proper distance. It is difficult to make a neat joint between the background and the outline of the form with rotary tools. Hand leveling with a flat iron tool and silicon-carbide grit mixed with water is often required to produce a clean boundary. Most relief carvings are small enough to hold in the hands against a fixed rotary tool in a stationary arbor, but some craftsmen prefer a hand-held machine, such as a flexible shaft or a small carver with a self-contained motor. In that case the work is held in a stationary position, and the tool moved against it. This is the only method for pieces that are too large to be manipulated with the hands. With either method an adequate supply of water is needed for lubrication.

Carving In-the-round

Carving in-the-round requires very careful planning and visualization of the design prior to execution. Although copying is to be discouraged in any creative work, it is useful as practice and training for craftsmen who have never previously attempted any form of sculpture. As a first project a small piece of sculpture such as a figurine, as simple in form as possible, can be used as a model. More advanced students and professionals prefer to design and make their own models in wax or modeling clay. The model is usually made the same size as the projected carving so that the dimensions can be measured directly from model to carving with a pair of sculptor's calipers. Some amateurs use a photograph of a selected object to project into a three-dimensional carving. This technique is more difficult than using a figure in-the-round as a model and is not recommended for beginners. Advanced carvers, however, often use a sketch of the design rather than a three-dimensional model. In either case it is usually necessary to draw patterns from several angles that are applied to the carving material as guides for blocking out the figure. One side and one end view may be sufficient, but often all four sides need to be developed (4-31). Each pattern should show the profile of the subject from its particular viewpoint. Make the patterns on strong paper and cut them out carefully along the outlines. Cement these patterns to the block of material in their relative positions. The block should be squared up with a slab or

trim saw to just over the outside dimensions of the carving. A copy of each pattern should be made to check progress in the later stages of the work after the originals have been carved away. It is a good idea to carefully draw around the outline of each pattern on the block with a waterproof, solventproof marker to provide a more permanent guide.

Depending on the size of the carving, either a trim saw or a slabbing saw or both can be used to block out the design. The cuts must be carefully planned to avoid cutting into the boundaries of the form. If you use a slabbing saw, you may have to wedge the piece in a vise to obtain the required angle for some of the cuts; an auxilliary clamp is also useful for this purpose. To cut away areas under the body and between the legs of an animal figure, for instance, it may be necessary to make multiple parallel cuts fairly close together and break out the standing pieces by wedging.

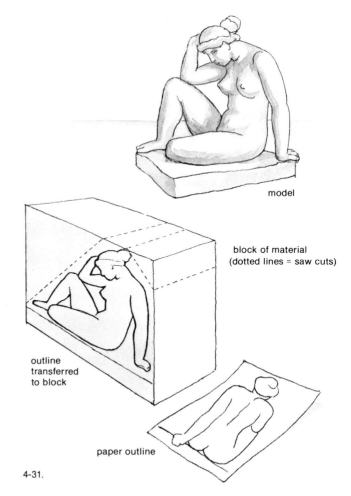

model

block of material
(dotted lines = saw cuts)

outline
transferred
to block

paper outline

4-31.

After the figure is blocked out as much as possible with the saw, it is ground. Again, depending on the size, grinding can be done with wheels 10″, 8″, or 6″, or smaller in diameter. In most cases, both large and small wheels are used: the larger wheels grind much faster, but the smaller wheels reach more areas. On a carving of appreciable size it is usually necessary to alternate between the two. A grinder that has worn down to about 4″ in diameter is often more useful than a larger one; a narrower wheel, than a broader one. Wheels 1/2″ and 1/4″ thick and 1″ to 3″ in diameter, mounted in the chuck of the carving machine, are excellent for roughing out even small carvings and for the second grinding stage after the figure is blocked out on a larger wheel. Still smaller wheels, mounted on 1/8″ and 3/32″ mandrels, can be used for further refinement and to reach recesses and depressions that are inaccessible to larger wheels. As areas are ground down to the outline, they should be marked. In further grinding they are avoided and serve as references for establishing other final points. When the figure is completely carved to within a fraction of its final dimensions, details can be added, such as lines, grooves, and textures. Tools for this stage of work are mounted wheels and points of silicon-carbide or diamond grit or homemade soft-iron tools used with loose abrasives (4-32). Water lubrication (4-33) is necessary except for soft-iron tools, with which a mixture of grit and water is applied to the work with the finger or a brush. Successively finer grits, from coarse 100- or 120-grit abrasive up to 400- or 500-grit, are used. A splash guard should be set up to protect the face. This procedure is similar in every respect to that used by Chinese carvers to obtain such magnificent results: only the machine and the source of power are different. Although preliminary carving with silicon-carbide and diamond tools is faster, there is no better method of carving small details and smoothing to a prepolish.

4-32.

After the form is completely developed with carving tools, sanding is begun. Several different techniques are usually required for the same carving because of irregularities such as openings, grooves, and recesses. Coarse sanding can usually be done with a standard sanding drum; the belt sander offers a variety of flat and curved surfaces that can work into many areas; but for small, tight contours in grooves and recesses smaller tools are required. They must be chosen individually to fit a particular area of the carving. As in regular sanding techniques, proceed from coarse to fine tools to achieve a good prepolish. Rubber wheels come in a variety of grades, as do miniature sanding drums, but there are a number of areas on most carvings into which even these

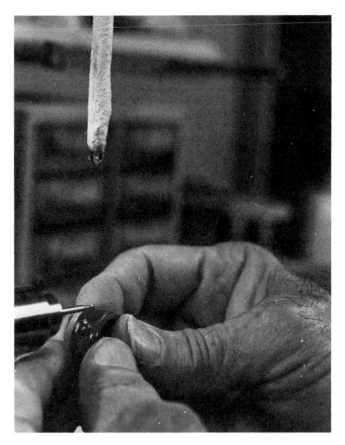

4-33.

tools will not fit. In such cases homemade soft-iron or wooden dowel-rod tools in special sizes must be used with loose abrasive grits. Many materials can be sanded in all but the most inaccessible places with muslin polishing buffs impregnated with wet abrasive grains. They must be started at a slow speed to avoid throwing the mixture off, but as the grit settles into the threads of the buff, higher speeds can be used effectively. Materials that undercut cannot be sanded by this method: they require tools with a firm surface such as leather, metal, or wood. Another method is to impregnate a buff with a weak solution of glue and roll it in grit while it is still wet. After it dries, it provides a more durable and resistant surface than plain water and grit alone but is not as easily renewed with fresh grit. Fine sanding that produces a prepolish and, on some materials, a final polish can be achieved with shellac wheels and points (see chapter 2).

Many craftsmen feel that every carving must be polished as highly as possible over its entire surface. Although this may be appropriate for some work, a richer and more interesting effect can be attained by contrasting highly polished areas with mat or semipolished surfaces. You must decide on the most suitable effect for each particular work. Polishing a carving to a mirrorlike finish differs from polishing any other piece only in the use of smaller wheels and points of various shapes to reach into places that are not accessible to the larger wheels. Since the materials used for carving vary just as for other types of lapidary work, you must select an effective polishing technique for the particular material you are using.

Carving Materials

Most gem materials that are solid and free from fractures, soft spots, and unsightly blemishes can be made into effective carvings. A thorough examination of the block of material before starting work is as important for carving as for hollow vessels: it is a crushing disappointment to spend time and effort in blocking out a carving in-the-round only to discover some hidden flaw that makes it totally unusable for the intended purpose. This is impossible to avoid at times, but the chance can be minimized by being extremely cautious: if you have a reasonable doubt about a given material at any stage of the work, it is better to discard it altogether than to run the risk involved.

Soft materials are easier to carve, but harder ones offer better possibilities for fine finish, precise detail, and crisp style. They are also more durable and less likely to fracture in carving or in use. The softer and less valuable materials are better choices for a first project. Relatively soft materials suitable for carving include alabaster,

4-34. *Falseface Figure*, Tuscarora steatite carving, 5 1/2" high, made by Duffy Wilson.

soapstone, serpentine, calcite, howlite, jet, coral, amber, and ivory. All of these can be carved easily with steel tools such as burrs, files, rasps, rotary and hand saws, knives, or chisels. Ivory, amber, and coral are more valuable and often used for jewelry. Most of the materials listed occur in large enough masses to be used for small sculpture.

Soft materials can be sanded by regular methods, but they tend to load up the cloth, particularly in dry sanding. They create a lot of dust, so you should wear a protective mask to avoid inhaling too much of it. A lot of work can be done easily by hand with a sanding cloth, which does not create a dangerous amount of dust. Most soft materials respond well to commonly used polishing agents and techniques, but, since they are generally more absorbent than denser materials, colored agents such as red rouge and chromium oxide often penetrate and stain them and should therefore be avoided. Tin oxide, pumice, and air-float tripoli are good choices. The cutting compound known as White Diamond, a white tripoli in bar form, is best for ivory.

Amber and ivory are among the most popular soft materials for carving. Amber is a fossil resin found in small lumps up to a few inches in diameter. It carves easily with hand tools but also tends to chip. It is difficult to use rotary tools for sanding and polishing amber because even moderate speeds cause the surface to melt and smear, and sanding cloth is quickly filled up with gum and stops cutting. The best sanding material is medium- or fine-grade pumice-powder paste. If it is used wet on a muslin buff, overheating is avoided. Final polishing is easily accomplished by using toothpaste on the buff and running at a slow speed.

4-35. Eskimo carved-ivory dance group, stone base, 3 3/8″ high, made by Peter Seeganna.

4-36. Cuff links, carved ivory, 14K gold.

4-37. Earrings, ivory, amber.

Ivory is perhaps the finest soft carving material. Although it is not a mineral, it is considered a lapidary material since it is often worked with lapidary techniques. It has been carved artistically by every culture to which it was available from prehistoric to modern times. Elephant tusks provide the largest blocks—up to 5″ in diameter at the butt and several feet in length. Prehistoric mammoths and mastodons left their tusks and skeletons in the soil, where they are often unearthed in mining operations. particularly in the Arctic. The ivory is perceptibly harder than modern ivory and is excellent for carving. The tusks are usually split in concentric layers so that large sections are seldom sound throughout. However, the layers are often sound in themselves and are normally 1/2″ or so thick, providing pieces of substantial size for carving. This ivory is sometimes stained by minerals in the soil to beautiful shades of earth reds, yellows, browns, and blue-black. Ancient walrus ivory is colored in the same way. Prehistoric ivory is usually called *fossil ivory*, although scientifically speaking it is not a fossil. It is not abundant and is difficult to obtain except in Alaska, but some dealers do sell it by mail (see appendix 3). Modern walrus tusks are not available legally from the Alaska source where most walruses are found. A federal law prohibits export in unworked form in order to preserve the supply for native Eskimo carvers. Some material was exported before this law was passed, but none is currently available through dealers. Elephant ivory can be obtained from a few commercial sources.

The best and fastest method of working ivory is with rotary steel tools, although the traditional method is with steel hand tools. Ivory cannot be worked fully or efficiently with diamond saws or with conventional grinding equipment. Steel saws can be employed for sectioning but must be run at a relatively slow speed to avoid burning the material. Rotary burrs can rough out a piece in a fraction of the time required by hand methods, and interesting textures can be produced with small burrs in special shapes, such as dental and metalwork burrs. Small rotary steel saws are also excellent, as are silicon-carbide cutoff disks. A drum-type grinding tool is particularly useful for the roughing-out process (4-38). The surface is similar to that of a nutmeg grater, and it can remove stock at a rapid rate. All of the steel tools that are suitable for ivory can also be used to carve the other soft materials listed above.

After the work is roughed out, it can be smoothed with regular dry-sanding cloth, emery paper, or ordinary sandpaper. Loose abrasive on a damp buff should not be used, as the grain becomes embedded in the surface of the ivory rather than abrading it. Full-size sanding equipment can be used on some pieces, but smaller drum sanders are more convenient for most work. Ivory should not be worked wet: it absorbs moisture and is inclined to crack when it dries out. Since a great deal of dust is created if ivory is worked dry with power tools, you should wear a protective mask over your mouth and nose or work in front of a dust collector connected to a blower. The author's setup for carving soft materials consists of both a high-speed machine for small-diameter tools, such as a steel burr (4-39) or a drum sander (4-40), and a full-size polishing motor for larger tools. They are mounted in front of a suction dust collector, and the dust is gathered in a compartment in the bench.

Ivory responds to almost any polishing technique, but the author recommends the white-tripoli bar known as White Diamond mentioned previously. This compound carries the abrasive in a grease base and combines cutting and polishing. The bar is pressed against the wheel while it is running, which loads it with the compound. When the tripoli is first applied to the ivory, the abrasive grains are sharpest, producing a cutting action. As the grains wear down, they begin to produce a finer finish and finally a high gloss. Tripoli cuts out any scratches left from sanding and can even round the forms slightly, which makes a perfect prepolishing unnecessary. Do not run the buff at high speed or exert too much pressure: this creates heat that will burn the surface and turn it brown.

4-38.

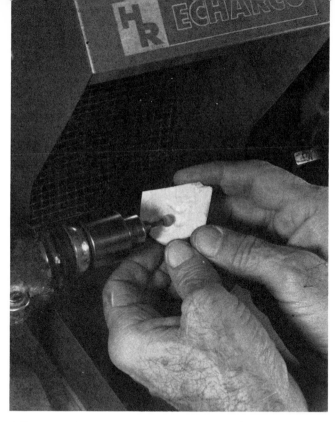

4-39.

4-40.

Methods of working ivory also apply to bone and other organic materials, such as tortoiseshell, hoof, horn, and baleen.

The following medium-hard materials can be carved with silicon-carbide tools and abrasive grains and with diamond tools: agate, jasper, obsidian, feldspar, rhodonite, turquoise, bowenite, malachite, opal, nephrite, jadeite, idocrase, crystalline quartz, tourmaline, garnet, beryl, and tigereye. Nephrite jade, because of its extreme toughness, is the ideal carving material, followed by jadeite and cryptocrystalline quartzes such as agate and jasper. Many other materials can also be carved: those listed here are the most common. Extremely hard materials, such as corundum—ruby and sapphire—can be efficiently worked only with diamond tools and abrasives.

Engraving

Gem engraving is a highly specialized technique. It demands great manual skill that can be acquired only by long, patient practice and application. In this respect it is similar to metal hand engraving, although quite different in technique. It is necessary to develop a very sensitive touch and to maintain it by continuous practice. Engraving tools are handmade soft-iron or copper rotary points and wheels in several shapes and sizes. They are charged with diamond grit and mixed with oil to prepare them for engraving. Silicon-carbide grit with oil or water may be used on stones less than 8 in hardness.

The engraving machine is always a stationary horizontal arbor. It must have a small, highly accurate chuck or draw-in collet. It must allow variable speeds to fit the requirements of different materials. Diamond-charged tools should be operated at high speeds on most hard materials so that a very light touch can be used to avoid dislodging the diamond charge. The smaller the diameter of the tool, the faster the speed should be: speeds up to 10,000 r.p.m. and higher are often desirable. The engraver sits comfortably in front of the bench-mounted machine. The hands must rest at the proper height to manipulate the work with the fingers. Small leather or canvas bags loosely filled with sand are used to steady the hands (2-43). They can be pushed into shape like pillows to rest the hands at the exact height required for each piece of work. For very small-scale work most engravers use a magnifier.

To charge the tools, the diamond grit is mixed with oil on an agate or jasper slab, using a toothpick. Olive oil is traditionally used both to mix the charge and to lubricate the cutting action, but light machine oil is just as good. Two or three different diamond-grit sizes, from medium- to fine-grade, may be used to charge the tools: the range from 45-micron (325-mesh) to 30-micron (600-mesh) is used for most of the cutting; 6-micron (3,000 mesh) to 1 micron (14,000 mesh), for polishing. (See the section on carving tools in chapter 2 for a description of turning soft-iron and copper tools to shape in the carving machine.) You will need a variety of shapes for engraving (2-61); some points may be smaller than the head of a pin. Very small tools are usually made of copper, which is softer than iron and takes a diamond-grit charge more readily. Light pressure should be exerted on soft-copper tools in charging to keep them from bending. Copper points are usually soldered onto steel shanks. The slab on which the diamond mixture is smeared is held against the slowly rotating tool. As much pressure as the tool will stand without bending is applied, causing the diamond grains to embed themselves in the surface. With proper charging and lubrication the tools will cut for some time before they need to be recharged.

The best method of laying out the design on the stone is to cover the polished surface with a coating of Chinese white, an opaque watercolor paint. The design can then be drawn on the coating with a sharp-pointed pencil. Guidelines are cut through the coating with a fine knife-edge point, then the painted coating is washed off and the rest of the engraving developed. Some craftsmen draw the complete design on the finely sanded but not polished surface of the stone and do the engraving without cutting preliminary guidelines. If the surface of the stone is polished after engraving, however, there is some danger of rounding the sharp edges of the design areas.

Proper engraving, called *intaglio*, is cutting a design below the surface of the surrounding material. Gem engraving, however, includes a few other styles (4-41). In *relievo* the background is lowered and the design stands out. This is simply miniature carving in relief. The *cameo*, cut in the relievo technique, is also classed as engraving. When this form was popular, many cameos were cut in stratified or banded agate, in which the layers are in contrasting colors. The darker layer of a two-colored stone was usually left as the background for the lighter color, although the reverse was also done. Layered agate of contrasting colors was occasionally used for intaglio as well. The designs were cut through one layer to reveal the contrasting color of the lower layer in the engraved areas. Most intaglio engravings were left unpolished, with a mat finish to contrast with the polished surface of the background. Shell cameos are considered a form of engraving, although the technique is quite different from stone engraving. Since shell material is quite soft, it can be carved more easily with steel hand tools than with rotary tools. Small knives and the gravers used on wood and metal are most efficient for this kind of work. *Chevet* combines intaglio and relievo in that the background is carved away to leave a surrounding rim that forms a frame for the figure. It protrudes slightly above the level of the engraved or carved figure, protecting it from wear. Another style of engraving is done in transparent or highly translucent materials by carving the design from the rear of the stone in intaglio. From the front the design, which appears in reverse, has the appearance of a relief carving floating in the material. The carving must be left with a mat finish to allow the modeling of the forms to be seen through the clear material. This technique is essentially the same as that employed in engraving crystal glassware from the inside, but the work is usually on a smaller scale.

Etching
Etching with acids gives a somewhat similar effect to very shallow surface engraving. Carbonate stones such as calcite can be etched with diluted hydrochloric acid, while silicates such as quartz and feldspar require full-strength hydrofluoric acid. The technique is similar to that used in etching metals. Asphaltum varnish is used as the resist. The stone must first be polished, then the design is drawn or painted on the surface with Chinese white to clearly show the areas to be etched. The black varnish is then carefully painted on the surface areas not to be attacked

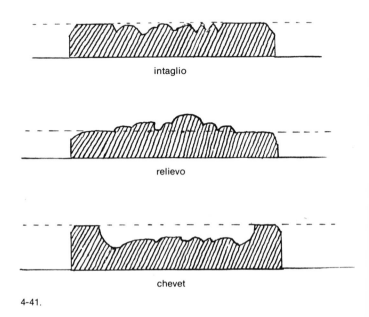

intaglio

relievo

chevet

4-41.

by the acid. When the varnish has dried thoroughly, the Chinese white is washed off and the article is submerged in the acid. The surface is dissolved and attains a soft, even dullness that contrasts beautifully with the high polish of the areas not touched by the acid. A 10- to 15-minute hydrofluoric-acid bath is usually required to achieve a good etched effect. Check the work continuously and remove it when the desired finish is achieved. The work should be done outdoors, since the fumes, particularly of hydrofluoric acid, are extremely corrosive and dangerous to both skin and lungs. Rubber gloves should be worn, and the work placed in the acid bath with a pair of long-handled tongs. The plastic or rubber bath vessel should be covered to contain the fumes. The etching need not be very deep: the piece should remain in the acid only long enough to produce a good mat finish.

Hand Cutting

The variety of effects that can be achieved by hand cutting is quite limited, but it is a good way to test your affinity for lapidary work before investing in more costly equipment. It is also a good method for fragile or heat-sensitive materials. Cabochons with rounded tops are the most common form, but flat stones and simple flat facets can be cut when you have developed some skill.

The only equipment you need is a small, medium-grit grindstone or piece of one (most lapidaries have a worn-out wheel or two to spare); some pieces of silicon-carbide wet-or-dry sanding cloth, 6″ or 8″ × 12″, in 120-, 220-, 320-, and 600-grit grades; a thin piece of smooth leather, 3″ or 4″ wide by 8″ or so long; dop sticks and dop wax; polishing compound; and a simple homemade canvas-covered wooden frame (4-42).

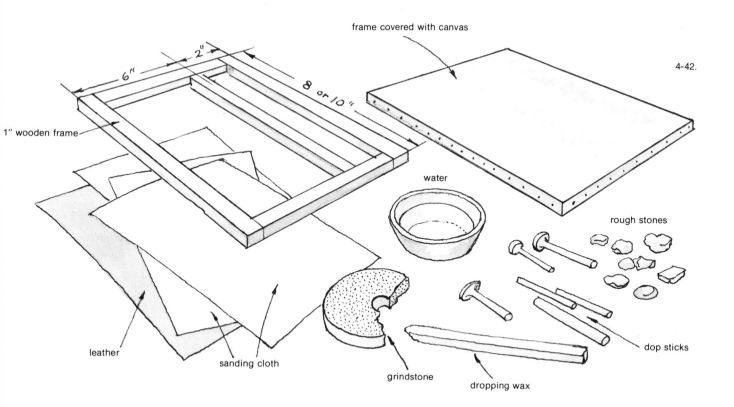

4-42.

frame covered with canvas

2″

6″

8 or 10″

1″ wooden frame

water

rough stones

leather

sanding cloth

grindstone

dropping wax

dop sticks

To begin, select a soft, easily polished material: turquoise, howlite, variscite, and serpentine are possibilities. Start with a piece of cut slab—a *blank*—the approximate size of the stone you wish to cut. Mark out the shape of the stone on the blank in the manner previously described. With most soft materials you can pinch off the edges fairly close to the outline with a pair of pliers, which will leave a rough edge that can easily be ground away and smoothed to an accurate contour. Do not grind the edge until the top of the stone has been ground, because it will then be thinner and easier to grind accurately. The blank is fastened to a short dop stick, and the grinder is laid flat on a table, bench, or other support at a convenient height. Pour water on the grinder and start working the stone across the face from side to side with a rotary movement, which will grind down the outer edges. Keep the grinding surface wet and turn the stone as you work to gradually form an evenly contoured crown, proceeding from the outer edges toward the center. More arm movement is required than for grinding with a rotary wheel in order to cover the entire curving crown of the stone. Keep working and testing the curve by eye until you have a perfect crown from all sides, then grind the final girdle profile.

Sanding is done on the canvas-covered frame. It has two open areas, wide and narrow, to accommodate different-size stones. The canvas or cloth is tacked flat to the frame across the upper face. A piece of coarse silicon-carbide cloth is laid on the canvas, and water is poured onto the surface. The stone is worked in one of the two open areas, depending on its size. The give of the canvas and the sanding cloth allows all areas of the face to receive contact while the stone is rubbed back and forth, which eliminates the small, flat irregularities inevitably left by grinding. Keep the sanding cloth wet at all times, and, as in regular sanding, change to finer grades of cloth as you proceed to the final prepolish stage. Polishing is done in the same way, substituting the leather strip for the sanding cloth. Use any polishing compound that is appropriate for the particular material. For flat stones and flat areas the sanding cloth and leather are attached to an absolutely flat, smooth base; otherwise the technique is exactly the same. If pebbles or other irregular fragments are used, the base must be ground flat on the grindstone before forming the top.

You will find the softer stones fairly easy to do. Harder materials require more time and patience but respond just as well to hand treatment. As mentioned in the beginning, soft and fragile stones can be more safely and sometimes more accurately contoured by the hand method than with standard equipment. It is a useful technique for professionals as well as for amateurs and hobbyists.

5. Applications

The application of human imagination to the beautiful materials proffered by the earth has produced large numbers of useful and artistic objects throughout history. It is difficult for the modern lapidary to discover or invent an article or a style that was not utilized sometime in the past. But contemporary designers should be open to the possibilities arising from changing lifestyles and to fresh approaches to old ideas. Lapidary is a medium that can be used just as effectively to express the aesthetics of the present as it has that of the past. The work of past generations is a fund of information and inspiration. The lapidary should become familiar with the history of the art and with its numerous examples. The ancient civilizations of Egypt

5-2. Chinese lion, jade, Han period (B.C. 206–220 A.D.).

5-1. Chinese censer, green jade, K'ang Hsi period (1662-1722).

5-3. Chinese bowl, green jade, Chien Lung period (1736-1795).

and China offer especially fertile areas for research, and the more primitive cultures of Central and South America give impressive testimony to the high level of perfection attainable without the use of elaborate mechanical equipment.

The various categories of lapidary work produced by past generations include the following: all forms of jewelry; freestanding and relief sculpture; inlay of all types, stone into metal, metal into stone, and surface treatment of sculptured pieces; relievo and intaglio engraving, as in seals and signets; hollow vessels of all kinds; mirrors (hematite); knives, forks, spoons, and other utensils; architectural panels; boxes and lids; candelabra; screens; gongs; musical instruments; wind chimes; translucent windows; handles for vessels, implements, and tools; cutting and piercing knives; weapons and handles; combs; escutcheon plates; buttons; hook-and-eye fasteners; belt buckles and belt hooks; beads; oil lamps; game boards; chessmen and other game pieces; pictorial compositions; plaques; manicure sets; smoking pipes; cigarette and cigar holders; and fishing lures. This list does not include industrial products such as gears and bearings for machines, burnishers, creasers, scrapers, drills, mortars and pestles, and mullers, most of which the creative lapidary is rarely concerned with. This chapter does describe a few useful tools that the craftsman can make for his shop. Most of the numerous applications of lapidary materials and skills have been ignored by modern craftsmen; only a few projects are described here. Other popular applications of lapidary techniques that are novelties rather than legitimate art forms are omitted. Except for the section on useful shop tools the applications that in the author's opinion offer the greatest creative possibilities are described. Many readers will discover or invent other creative ways to utilize lapidary materials and techniques. The examples are offered simply as a starting point for the development of original ideas.

5-4. Ancient Egyptian necklace (detail), gold, lapis lazuli, carnelian, turquoise, green feldspar.

5-5. Mayan (600–900 A.D.) figurine, jadeite, carved in relief, 8″ high.

5-6. Olmec (c. 500 B.C.) carved head, jadeite, 2 5/8" high.

5-7. Eskimo silver bracelet, ivory, jade inlay, made by Jerry Norton.

5-8. Eskimo pendant, fossil-ivory, ebony inlay, made by Peter Seeganna.

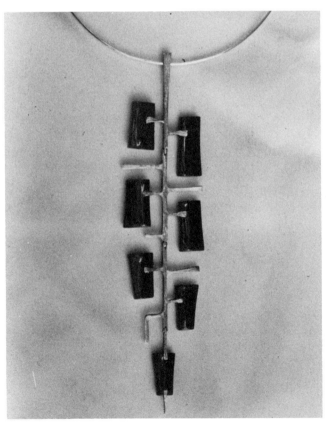

5-9. Pendant necklace, green jade, 14K gold.

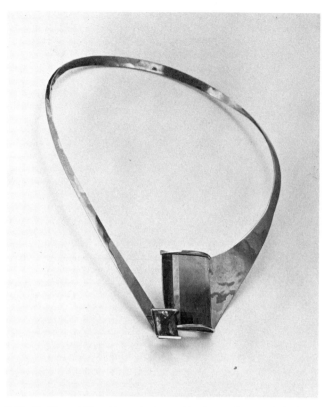

Jewelry

Of all the uses to which lapidary materials and techniques have been applied jewelry is by far the most popular. For this reason one might expect jewelers to be more concerned with designing and cutting gemstones than anyone else—why this is not true is discussed in the preface to this book. The creative jeweler should realize how advantageous even the most basic knowledge and skill in lapidary can be. With the skill to produce a stone of any desired shape in any chosen material the jeweler can create a design without having to conform to the restrictions of standard commercially fabricated stones. The sensitive designer is certain to appreciate and profit by this freedom: he can conceive and create more personal, better-integrated designs; he can develop a more innovative attitude; he can invent new shapes, new ways of combining metal and stone. Even amateur and hobbyist jewelers may discover the satisfaction of producing unique stones and lose interest in cutting stereotypes with standard templates.

5-10. Necklace, 14K gold, smoky topaz, blue tourmaline, made by Irena Brynner, stones by Francis J. Sperisen.

5-11. Ring, black jade, Australian opal, 14K gold.

5-12. Santo Domingo Pueblo shell pendant, coral, mother-of-pearl, turquoise, jet mosaic inlay.

5-13. Silver bracelet, turquoise inlay, made by Victor Glover.

5-15. Hopi ring, silver, turquoise, inlay on band, made by Louis Mojica.

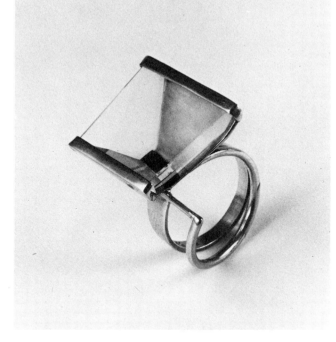

5-14. Ring, white gold, quartz, made by Margaret de Patta, stone by Francis J. Sperisen.

5-16. Navajo bracelet, silver, turquoise.

Standardized gemstone shapes and cuts require standard setting methods. Variations and modifications are possible, but within rather narrow limits. On the other hand, stones can be shaped to fit into specially designed seats and sockets in the metal, and notches can be cut for arbitrarily arranged posts that hold the stone in place. Stones can be drilled for posts that extend to the surface and become part of the design (5-17).

Most jewelers think in terms of metal: if stones are included, they are usually contained in metal settings. Small stones may merely embellish the metal; larger stones may dominate it as the focal point of the design. Lapidaries, on the other hand, tend to think primarily in terms of gem materials and use metal only as a framework. Indian jewelry offers striking examples of both viewpoints. The Navajos, who until comparatively recently purchased their stones from traders or dealers, emphasize heavy metalwork with few if any stones. The opposite is true of the Zunis, who cut all their own gems. They use many stones in a variety of techniques, all of which feature a lavish display of gem materials. It is possible and practical even to utilize gem materials as the basic structure of the piece, employing metal only for accent, for connecting and unifying elements of the design, or for *findings* (the elements that attach the piece to the wearer.) Metal can even be excluded completely, as a bracelet made entirely of organic materials, which takes advantage of their springiness to hold the circular shape under tension when it is clasped (5-22).

5-18. Interlocking engagement-wedding rings, black jade, ivory, 18K yellow gold.

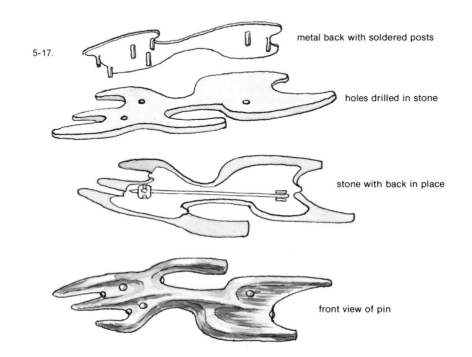

5-17.

metal back with soldered posts

holes drilled in stone

stone with back in place

front view of pin

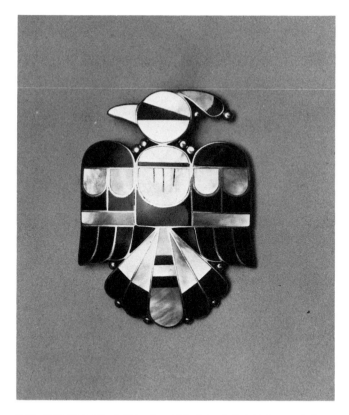

5-19. Zuni silver pin, mother-of-pearl, tortoiseshell, jet inlay, made by Myra Tuscon.

5-21. Zuni Pueblo silver pin, jet, mother-of-pearl, turquoise, coral intarsia-type inlay.

5-20. Zuni Pueblo silver pin, turquoise clusterwork.

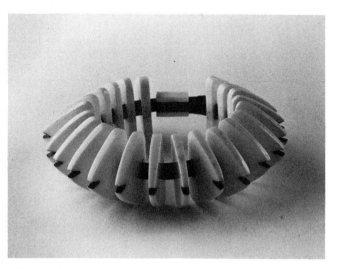

5-22. Bracelet, walrus ivory, baleen.

Bracelets with solid links can be made by cutting hinges directly in the gem material (5-23). Any of several types of joints, basically tongue-and-groove or dovetail, can be used and held together with metal hinge-pins inserted in holes drilled laterally through the joints. Stainless-steel pins are best for this purpose, as they will withstand wear for a very long time. Only the ends of the pins will show, but they can be hidden if desired by capping with gold or silver plugs just long enough to be scored and held in place with epoxy. For watch bracelets holes can also be drilled in the material to accept the spring bars that hold the watch to the bracelet. Necklaces can be engineered in much the same manner, except that the joints must be flexible in two directions in order to fit around the neck and conform to the curve of the shoulders and breast. The easiest and least wasteful way to obtain curved links for bracelets is to cut out a solid band with a core drill and to cut it apart into sections. With more labor and slightly more waste the links can be cut out of a flat slab of adequate thickness, and the curves ground on top and bottom (5-26). The materials for hinged brace-lets and necklaces must be chosen with care, and the hinges must be strong enough not to break under normal stress and shock. Nephrite jade is the most shock-resis-tant gem material. Ivory, although a much softer material, is also tough and resilient, as are tortoiseshell, hoof, and horn. Quartz-family minerals, such as agate and jasper, and jadeite should be practical if they have suf-ficiently thick joints.

Solid circlet bracelets and rings are practical only in nephrite. Jadeite was also used by the Chinese, but it fractures more easily than nephrite. To overcome this tendency, the Chinese made these bracelets round in crosssection as well as in outline, and the material was at least 1/2" thick. If the wearer is reasonaby careful, this type of bracelet will last indefinitely; but if it is dropped or struck a hard blow, it will fracture or break apart. A similar nephrite bracelet is almost indestructible in normal use.

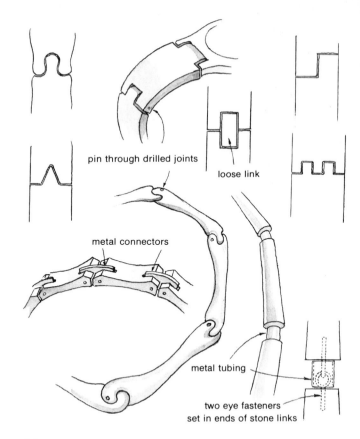

pin through drilled joints

loose link

metal connectors

metal tubing

two eye fasteners set in ends of stone links

5-23.

5-24. Bracelet, carved green jade, gold hinges.

96

5-25. Black-jade watch bracelet.

Color plates on pages 98 and 99.

C-1. Zuni silver ring, ironwood, turquoise, shell, jet inlay, made by Roger Tsabetsaye.

C-2. Silver pendant, malachite, shell-heishi, coral, walnut, satinwood, turquoise inlay, made by Mary Ann Nibbelink.

C-3. Pendant necklace, black jade, 14K-gold-cast inlay.

C-4. Bracelet, mammoth ivory, baleen inlay.

C-5. 14K-gold bracelet, black-coral, ivory, turquoise inlay, inset diamond, made by Steve Ballard.

C-6. Silver belt buckle, turquoise, ironwood inlay, made by Curt Pfeffer.

C-7. Black-jade ring, 14K-gold-cast inlay.

C-8. Silver bracelet, turquoise, ironwood, coral inlay, made by Curt Pfeffer.

C-9. *Winter Germination*, silver bracelet, ivory, serpentine, malachite, turquoise, ironwood, ebony inlay, made by Eveli.

C-10. 14K-gold wedding rings, black-jade, turquoise inlay.

C-11. Navajo silver hinged box, turquoise, shell mosaic inlay on lid, made by Jimmie Herald.

C-12. Mazdaliths, internally lighted wall panels, 50″ high, 12″ wide, made by Dee Church.

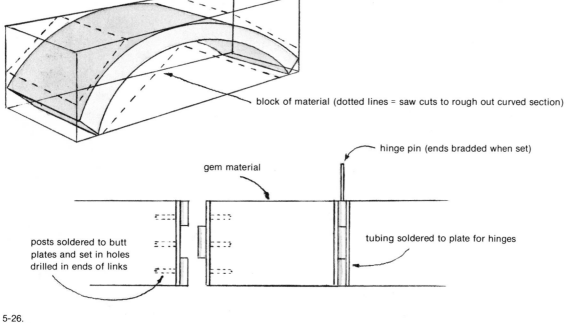

block of material (dotted lines = saw cuts to rough out curved section)

hinge pin (ends bradded when set)

gem material

posts soldered to butt plates and set in holes drilled in ends of links

tubing soldered to plate for hinges

5-26.

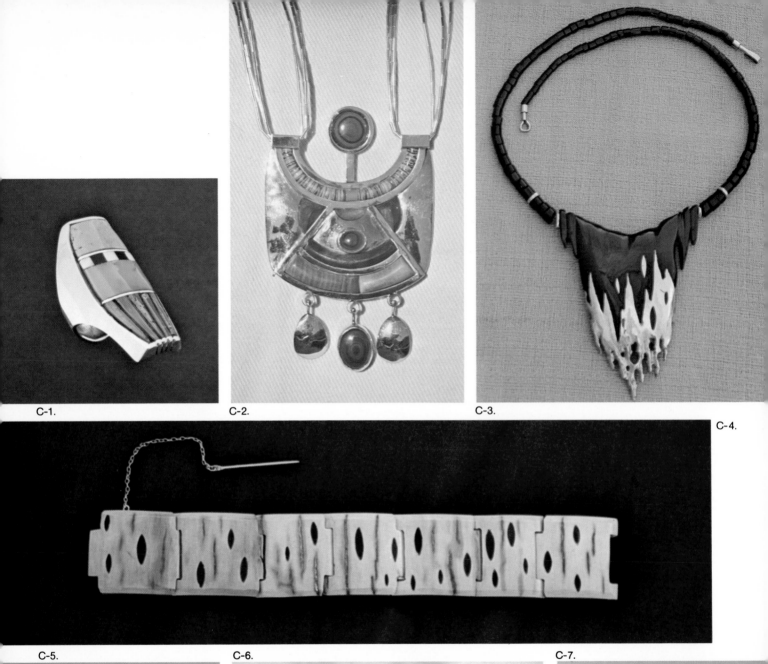

C-1.

C-2.

C-3.

C-4.

C-5.

C-6.

C-7.

C-8.

C-10.

C-9.

C-11.

C-12.

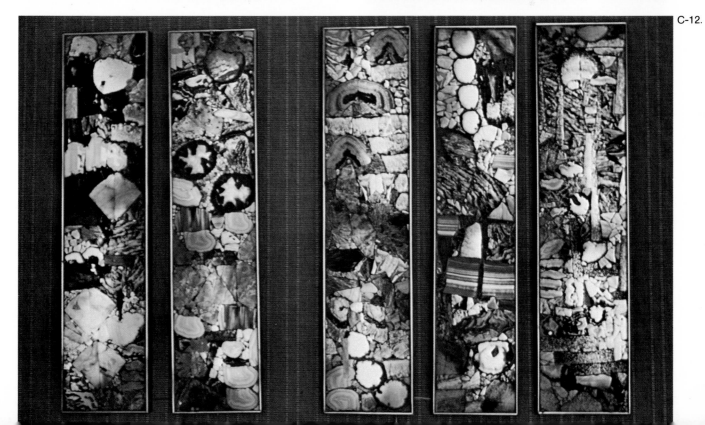

Solid nephrite-jade band rings are also very practical. They can be further strengthened by lining and edging with metal, particularly 10K or 14K gold. The liner and the edges can be constructed so that the connection between them does not show and the metal appears to be all of one piece (5-27). A perfect result depends on careful execution of each step of the process. The bands must fit over the liner precisely; they must be beveled smoothly at the proper angle; the liner must be flared and burnished tightly against the bevel; and the joint must be polished at right angles. Tripoli and a miniature soft muslin buff are used for polishing, since some cutting is needed to hide the joint. Yellow rouge run at a high speed can be used for the final finish. The bands can also be made without liners, or the liner can be simply flared and burnished over the slightly beveled inner edge of the band, but the edges will be thin, without the substantial, tailored appearance of the attached bands, which can be as heavy as desired (5-28). For the liner use 28-gauge 10K or 14K gold sheet or 26-gauge sterling silver, which is more malleable than gold. White gold is too hard and springy; heavier gauges of yellow gold or silver are more difficult to flare. However, 26-gauge gold and 24-gauge silver give a more substantial effect if no bands are used. A lightweight, domed-face planishing hammer is used to help flare the metal, and a flat-face hammer to bring it in contact with the edge of the nephrite-jade band. The metal must be fully annealed before starting. To finger-size the jade band, allow three-quarters of a size of the thickness of the liner with 28-gauge metal, a full size with 26-gauge, and one and one-quarter size with 24-gauge. This varies slightly depending on whether the finger size is small or large, and the safest method is to make the liner to the exact size and then grind the inside of the jade band if necessary to form a perfect fit over the liner. The liner should be set in place with epoxy so that it will not move while being flared. The bands are cored out of the material as described in chapter 3.

A ring of unique construction is made with a thin band of jade enclosed in a shell of gold (5-29). The band is made perfectly flat and cylindrical and is polished inside and out. It can be as thin as 1/16″ because it is well protected by the surrounding metal. All surfaces of the band except the inside and one edge are covered with a layer of melted hard carving wax. After the wax is worked down to a layer of even thickness, the design openings are carefully cut out, and the jade band is removed from the open end of the wax shell. The wax is invested and cast in gold in the regular manner. (Silver can also be used.) After casting, a band of 28-gauge gold sheet the exact diameter of the cast ring is soldered to the open end. It should be

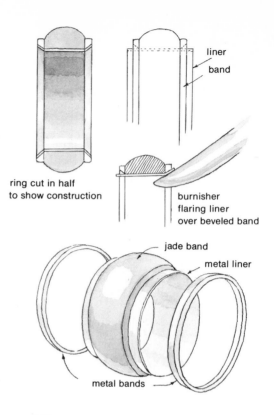

ring cut in half
to show construction

liner
band

burnisher
flaring liner
over beveled band

jade band
metal liner

metal bands

5-27.

5-28. Group of band rings, jade, 14K gold.

5-29. Band ring, jade, 14K-gold overlay.

wide enough to cover the edge of the ring when it is forced over it. The jade band is inserted in the casting and the soldered-on band is gradually forced over it by tapping around the edge with a light planishing hammer. The band must be gradually tapped evenly all the way around the edge; any tendency to wrinkle must be avoided by keeping an even circle of metal at all times as it is forced to a smaller diameter toward the center. If the metal is tapped properly, it will eventually lie perfectly flat against the edge of the jade band. It is then filed smooth, and the entire ring is polished (5-30).

Color plates on pages 102 and 103.

C-13. Zuni silver bracelet, jet, turquoise, shell inlay, made by Roger Tsabetsaye.

C-14. *Feathered Snake*, bracelet, fossil-ivory mosaic-type inlay, turquoise, diamond, made by Eveli.

C-15 and C-16. Inside and outside views of Hopi silver bracelet, turquoise, abalone, gold inlay, made by Louis Mojica.

C-17. Jade belt buckle, 24K-gold inlay.

C-18. Pin, jade, 14K-gold cast.

C-19. Round silver box, walnut, turquoise, malachite, lapis lazuli, serpentine, ivory, chrysocolla, shell, jet inlay, made by Bill Nibbelink.

C-20. Belt buckle, jade, gold accents.

C-21. Paneled agate window (detail), St. Mark Presbyterian Church, San Angelo, Texas, designed by W. C. Ray.

C-22. Necklace, ivory, baleen, turquoise, gold.

C-23. Necklace, red and yellow 14K gold, buffalo horn, walrus ivory, turquoise, made by Steve Ballard.

C-24. Walrus-ivory necklace, caribou-hoof inlay and appendages.

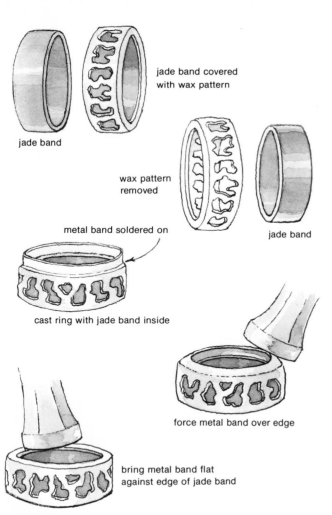

jade band

jade band covered with wax pattern

wax pattern removed

jade band

metal band soldered on

cast ring with jade band inside

force metal band over edge

bring metal band flat against edge of jade band

5-30.

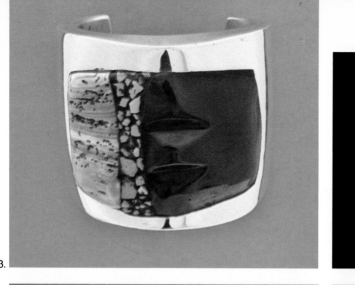

C-13.

C-14.

C-15.

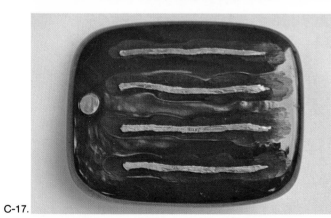

C-16.

C-17.

C-18.

C-19.

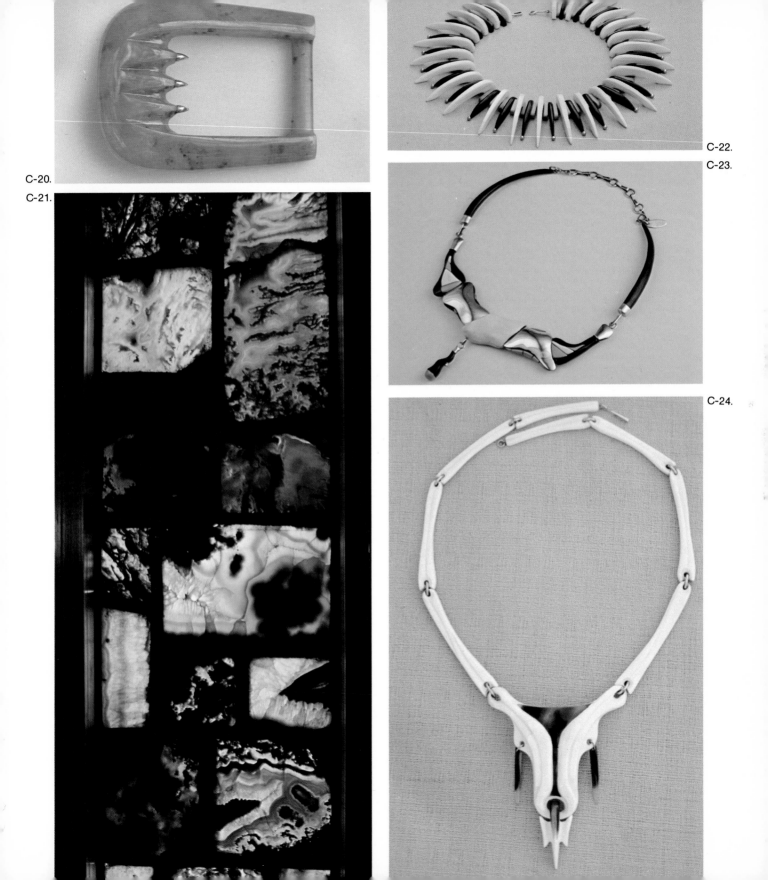

C-20.

C-21.

C-22.

C-23.

C-24.

Other jewelry applications in which gem material can be used as the body of the piece include pins (brooches), pendants, necklaces, earrings, cuff links, bola ties, belt buckles, barrettes—virtually every form of jewelry. Construction of most of these will require some type of carving. Pins offer many opportunities for inventive design, since there are no structural requirements except that they should lie flat, be relatively lightweight, and include some means of fastening to the garment. Metal can be used to back a carved design and hold the catch, for example; the back can also be held in place by reverse bezels, which enter and flare around the walls of tapered openings (5-31).

Button-type earrings and cuff links can be designed in various ways to utilize the stone as the basic material. To avoid a bezel and a metal back, the stone may be drilled and set on a post attached to the finding, which may or may not extend completely through the stone. If not, the finding can be cemented in place if the post is scored deeply enough for the cement to hold. Lapidary epoxy is relatively reliable, but it is doubtful that any epoxy is adhere to metal permanently unless it is applied under controlled temperature, humidity, and cleanliness conditions. It does adhere reliably to the stone, however, and the metal post cannot loosen if the epoxy is keyed solidly into the scored recesses.

To apply an accent or decorative element to the face of the stone, mount it on a metal tube and cement the tube in the drill hole first (5-35). The post attached to the earring finding is then inserted and cemented into the tube with epoxy. Even though two metal surfaces are cemented together, the scored post, the friction fit, and the fact that no strain is exerted on the parts assure a permanent attachment. The opposite procedure is followed for cuff links, which require greater strength at the point of attachment. A scored heavy-walled tube is soldered to the cuff back, or swivel joint, and the decorative element is soldered to a post, which is inserted and cemented in the tube.

Belt buckles can be made primarily of gemstone materials if they are properly designed to ensure strength (5-37). The entire buckle, including the tongue and belt loop, can be made of nephrite.

5-32. Cuff links, green jade, cast yellow-gold ornaments set in carved recesses.

5-31. Carved-jade pin.

5-33. Cuff links, green jade, 14K-yellow-gold inlay.

Pendants and bola ties are especially suitable for featuring gem material with few or no metal elements. Machine-made chains are usually not aesthetically suitable for hanging pendants—snake chain is a possible exception. Various other solutions can be tastefully and effectively employed, such as leather thongs, black nylon cords, plain metal bands, or hoops. The jeweler may also design and fabricate a suspension to harmonize with and extend the design of the pendant. It can be carried out in metal or in the pendant material. Gem-material beads in various shapes can be designed to serve as a chain, and chain links can be forged or fabricated by metal techniques.

5-34. Earrings, green jade, gold ornaments.

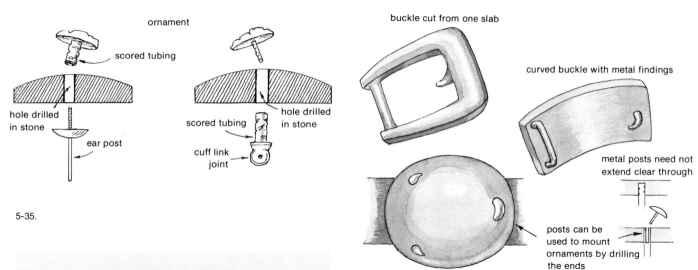

5-35.

5-37.

5-36. Belt buckle, green jade, 24K-gold inlay.

105

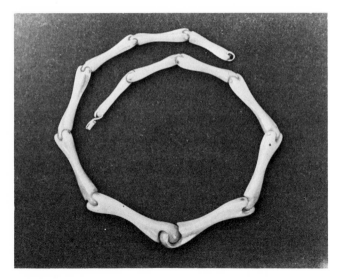

5-38. Necklace, pale-green jade, gold hinge pins and clasp.

Bola ties, so popular in the West, offer the same opportunities for creating pieces composed of or featuring gem materials. The tips that finish the ends of the cord can often be made of the gem material featured in the bola ornament. Since styles in men's jewelry have become much less inhibited recently, inventive possibilities have widened enormously. In addition to bola ties, pendants, bracelets, collar ornaments, brooches, hatbands and ornaments, shoe buckles, and even earrings may become common elements of male attire in the near future. The lapidary-jeweler will have an advantage over the metalworker, as he does in more traditional forms of jewelry.

5-39. Necklace, green jade, 14K yellow gold.

5-40. Bola tie, green jade, 14K-yellow-gold ornament.

Sculpture

Sculpture was once known as the plastic art and applied only to carved or modeled forms. Today almost any three-dimensional artwork is classed as a form of sculpture. This use of the word is largely a matter of convenience, since there is no more appropriate term to designate the tremendous range of unorthodox forms that are produced and exhibited today. The watchword is freedom from the inhibiting criteria of the past. The new sculpture includes all sorts of assemblage, collage, and constructions consisting of whatever materials or objects the artist selects to create an aesthetic statement. This is a field in which lapidary materials and techniques may be used imaginatively and with great effect. The craftsman-lapidary cannot only produce sculpture, particularly miniature forms, in the traditional sense of the word, but he also has the option of creating a wide variety of assemblages in which lapidary materials play an important role. He may combine them with wood, metal, or any other materials that fit the design and heighten the effect. He can embed

5-42. Carving, walrus ivory, walnut base, 12" high.

5-41. *Kneeling Man*, Cherokee steatite carving, 5" high, made by Julius Wilnoty.

5-43. Table piece, green jade, red agate, aluminum frame, serpentine base, 7 3/4" high, 10 3/4" wide.

107

or inlay gem material into a basic structure of wood, metal, or stone; he can set thin sections of translucent stone into apertures cut in the framework; he can suspend slabs of stone from crossarms or projections to create mobiles. These and other techniques can be used to construct wall pieces, table pieces, and other freestanding and hanging forms. This is a wide-open, unexplored contemporary field. The possibilities are endless, limited only by the creative imagination and technical proficiency of the lapidary.

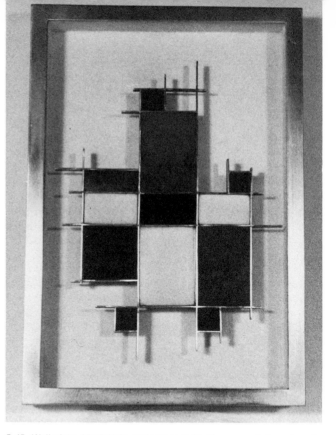

5-45. Wall piece, black jade, gray-green jade, blue-green jade, red agate, walrus ivory, silver framework, 8 1/4" high, 5 5/8" wide.

5-44. Wall piece, jasper, malachite, chrysocolla, serpentine, morrisonite, obsidian, common opal, sandstone background, 14" high, 10" wide.

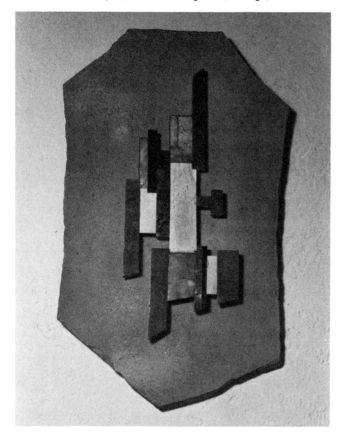

5-46. Table piece, green-jade picture slab, dark-green-jade base, gold accents, 8" high, 2 1/4" wide.

Screens

The application of gem materials to fixed or movable screens is just as feasible as it is to wall or table pieces. The frame structure of the screen may be metal or wood. If it is a solid-panel construction, the thin slabs of gem material can be cemented to the base with epoxy to form the design. Either or both sides can be treated, depending on how the screen is to be used. If the gem materials are predominantly opaque, reflected light will reveal the color and pattern; if translucent materials are used, a transmitted-light effect can be achieved by coating the backing with bright metal foil before applying the slabs. This will reflect light through the translucent stone. The structure of the screen may also be an open frame, without a backing, surrounding panels of translucent materials. In this case the free passage of light from both sides will reveal the full color and pattern of the materials. Many other structural- and surface-design possibilities can be investgated by the inventive designer (5-47).

One practical consideration is the fact that in a solid, overall surface treatment a great many slabs of gem material will be required for areas of even fairly modest dimensions. This can prove prohibitive in time and materials cost for many projects. One solution is to surround and intersperse the gem slabs with background areas of a neutral, nongem material. White plexiglass sheet, the same thickness as the gem slabs, can be employed effectively and inexpensively, and the edges of the the two materials will bond together perfectly with epoxy. This treatment may result in greater color emphasis through contrast, and very striking design effects are possible. Gem panels can also be set in blank areas of other materials. Clear plexiglass or plate glass can be used both for this purpose and for background material and give entirely different optical effects. An inventive design can also be employed for the structure of the screen, but if you are not familiar with wood and metal construction techniques, you should consult with professionals in these fields to ensure that your designs are structurally feasible.

For panel treatment a full-scale pattern should be drawn on strong paper and fastened to a level, smooth, horizontal backing. The slabs are cut precisely to fit this pattern and each other (see the sections on inlay and its derivatives in Chapter 4). The slabs should be cut the same thickness, and the surfaces polished (5-48). They are assembled by cementing the edges with epoxy, using a sheet of paper as a base. The paper is easily removed after the epoxy has set. The edges of the slabs should be coated with the adhesive and joined evenly. Wipe off excess adhesive while you work to avoid a difficult cleanup job later. Be sure to use a slow-setting lapidary epoxy, which allows up to 30 minutes of working time. The maximum strength is not reached until 7 days after application, but it becomes strong enough to handle after 24 hours at room temperature or 30 minutes under a heat lamp. If the design includes thin outlines dividing the slabs, the epoxy can be colored and opaqued by adding a

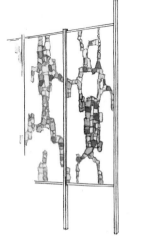

5-47.

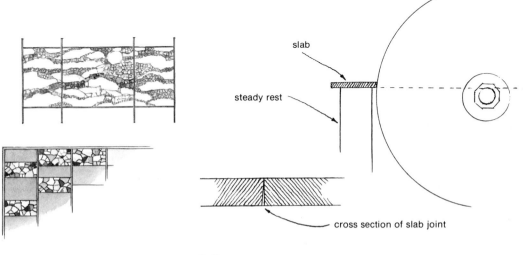

5-46.

small amount of dry pigment to the mixture. The pigment will not materially reduce the strength or adhesiveness of the cement. Epoxy is very tenacious even on polished surfaces, but any excess can be scraped away with a sharp, chisel-shaped blade. Don't forget to clean the rear side, where the epoxy adheres to the paper backing. After the panels are assembled, the epoxy cured, and the surfaces cleaned, they are fitted into the appropriate openings in the framework of the screen. They should fit snugly and can be fastened securely in place with narrow, inconspicuous wood or metal moldings.

Windows

Screen techniques can be used to create windows that resemble stained glass in the effect of transmitted light, although the colors are far more subtle. Brilliant colors occur in some materials such as jade and red and yellow agate, but muted colors predominate in decorative stones. You can also combine colored glass and gem materials to create effects unobtainable with either material alone. Gem materials are most effectively applied to comparatively small openings seen at a relatively close range, such as in vestibules, small rooms, or hallways. At such distances the colors and patterns found in materials such as moss, plume, and fern agate can be fully appreciated.

Because of the subtlety of gem materials the heavy leading used in regular stained-glass work is not appropriate for most designs. The slabs can be cemented edge to edge with epoxy, which is equally permanent for indoor or outdoor work since it is impervious to moisture, acids, and changing temperatures. Although the author knows of no outdoor gemstone windows of this type, experience with freestanding panels treated in this manner indicates that there is no reason why they should not be practical. The stone-to-stone joints are almost as resistant to pressure and breakage as the stone itself and should withstand normal wind pressures over areas of several square feet. The author recommends that the slabs be cut at least 3/16" thick, and the joints staggered for maximum structural strength. They should fit closely, but extreme precision is not advisable, as the epoxy is stronger in appreciable thicknesses than in thin films.

Using regular stained-glass leading as a framework for the slabs is by no means ruled out, as the jade window in the Kraft Chapel of the North Shore Baptist Church in Chicago proves (5-49). Leading was also used to construct the agate windows in the St. Mark Presbyterian Church, San Angelo, Texas, though the panels are only 6" wide (5-50).

Tabletops

Tabletops offer an excellent opportunity to use slabbed gem materials as surface treatment. The possibilities are many and varied, ranging from inlay through mosaic, intarsia, and parquetry (see the section on pictorial compositions later in this chapter).

Several approaches to the inlay are possible. A wood tabletop may be used as the plane of the surface with the

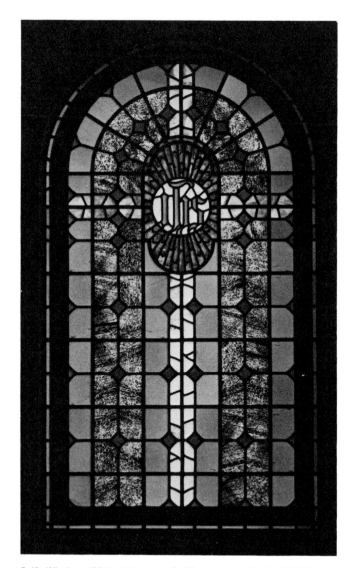

5-49. Window, 466 leaded panes of different-colored jade, 6 1/2' high, 3 1/2' wide, designed by Benjamin Franklin Olson, architect, for the North Shore Baptist Church, Chicago, James L. Kraft, donor.

decorative elements sunk into it flush with the surface. The wood must be routed out to the depth of the slabs to be embedded so that they will form a continuous level surface with the tabletop plane. The wood surface becomes an important element in the overall design, forming a background that unifies the pattern. It should be carefully finished before cutting and routing the beds for the stone slabs, which should likewise be polished before setting them in place with epoxy.

The above treatment requires more woodworking

5-50. Agate windows, St. Mark Presbyterian Church, St. Angelo, Texas, center panel 30' high, 6" wide, designed by W. C. Ray.

ability than an overall pattern of stone slabs, in which the surface does not have to be routed for individual units. In the latter case the entire tabletop is covered with stone. Which edge treatment is used depends on the material of the table itself—whether it is plastic, glass, wood, or metal. A molding of the appropriate material can be used to contain and reinforce the edge of the tabletop surface. It may be kept flush with the surface, project slightly above as a rim, or overlap. In installing the top make sure that the base is flat, level, and even and that the slabs are all the same thickness. The slabs are cut to fit face up on an accurate paper-outline pattern. The bed is covered with a coating of epoxy, starting with an area in the upper-left corner that is large enough for several pieces of material. The edges of these pieces are coated, applied, and fitted one by one. Adjacent areas are coated and the slabs removed from the paper design and applied until the whole top is completed.

If the slabs are not equally thick or if the base surface is rough and irregular, a paper pattern of the design in reverse must be made. The slabs are cut and fitted on this pattern face down. They are cemented edge to edge with epoxy, and the whole panel must set until thoroughly cured. A heavy mastic adhesive (a tile-setting adhesive will serve) is used to coat the base and the back of the slab panel and is worked into the irregularities. The entire panel is then lifted, turned over, and installed on the base. With this method the face will be level and smooth in spite of the unevenness of the back if the surface on which the slabs are assembled on the paper pattern is true. The last step is to remove the paper pattern and scrape away any excess adhesive. Solid stone panels can be surfaced and polished after assembly rather than polishing each piece beforehand. This requires an overhead rotary polisher that can be moved over the entire surface. This tool ensures a perfectly level, even surface with a minimum of effort but is rather expensive. Unless you flat-polish many large surfaces, the cost is hardly justifiable.

There is one method of constructing a tabletop with slabs that eliminates a great deal of time-consuming labor in polishing. The design is assembled in the manner previously described, but the slabs are not highly polished, and a sheet of plate glass is installed as the final surface. It is held in place by a molding that fits over and covers the entire thickness of the edge. The thickness of the glass is not apparent: the effect is of an evenly polished slab top. Glass is reasonably durable, and it can be repolished or replaced if it becomes dull or scratched. But the purist craftsman may with some justification reject this method as merely a convenient substitute for professional lapidary technique. One of the attractions of a gem-material surface is the durability and beauty of its finely polished finish. For this reason alone the popular embedding of slabs in plastic for tabletops is a poor alternative to the more craftsmanlike techniques.

Boxes

Wooden boxes and chests can be inlaid with gem materials by using the same techniques as for tabletops (5-51). They can be made by constructing a metal frame, into which solid gem slabs are inserted to form top, sides,

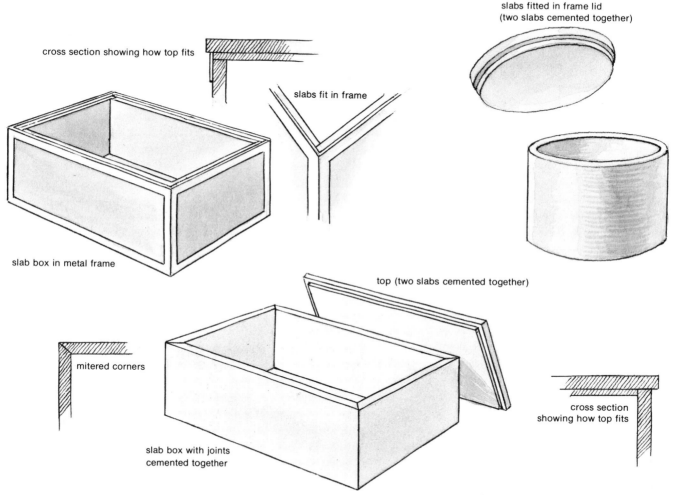

cross section showing how top fits

slabs fit in frame

slab box in metal frame

slabs fitted in frame lid
(two slabs cemented together)

mitered corners

top (two slabs cemented together)

slab box with joints
cemented together

cross section
showing how top fits

5-51.

and bottom. They can also be fabricated entirely of stone by cutting slabs to precise dimensions and assembling them as you would a wooden box. The pieces are cemented together with epoxy: no other reinforcement is necessary. A craftsmanlike effect is achieved by mitering the joints. It is difficult to cut precise angles for this purpose on a diamond saw: use a flat lap with a jig to hold the slab at a 45° angle for grinding. Round boxes can be made by cutting out a hollow cylinder with hole saws. The bottom can be fitted inside the cylinder and cemented; the top can be ground with a lip to fit inside the opening at the top of the cylinder. Many other designs and constructions are possible.

Hollow Forms

Awe-inspiring examples of hollow gem-material forms are found in Chinese work of almost every period. The technical mastery of jade carving exemplified by the range of these pieces, from tremendous wine bowls to tiny snuff bottles, is almost incredible. Hardly less unbelievable are the feats of carving performed by the pre-Columbian American cultures with far less sophisticated equipment. Most of the techniques used by primitive lapidaries are unknown, but it seems certain that the basic principles were the same as those used today. Indians of the Americas (and the Chinese before they developed iron tools) used bamboo cylinders as core drills to make hollow vessels. Bamboo grows in all diameters up to 1'. It wears down faster than metal when used as a drill, but its pores hold the abrasive grit better. The exact construction of the rotary machines used can only be conjectured. (Modern machines and methods of hollowing are discussed in the preceding chapter.)

The design of a hollow form is far more important than its mechanical perfection. No matter how perfectly finished a bowl or vase may be, a clumsy shape with unrefined contours will not give aesthetic satisfaction. Before undertaking a project that requires so much time and expensive material, concentrate on evolving an outstanding design. The subtleties of Chinese and pre-Columbian vessels, as well as ceramic and metal forms from other cultures, including contemporary work, should be studied, not to find something to copy but to analyze their artistry. They provide a background on the basis of which an original idea can be created.

Wall Decorations

Both interior and exterior walls can be used to support decorative installations. Such a decorative treatment may resemble masonry rather than lapidary work—for instance, raw pebbles utilized for textural effect, with color

of secondary importance. This field has not yet been investigated by lapidaries, but a knowledge of decorative colored stones and appropriate techniques opens up many possibilities that other craftsmen are not aware of. Panels that are flush with the surface of the wall can be treated with a mosaic technique, using either fixed boundaries or a vignette effect. Textural variety can be achieved by using natural pebbles as a contrasting background to polished surfaces. Some areas can be raised in high-relief, others positioned on differing planes, even recessed into the wall. Highly colored slag glass can be used to accent more muted tones, as can metals such as bronze, copper, brass, or stainless steel. The possibilities are almost limitless, and materials and methods used are dictated solely by the creativity of the designer and the effect he wishes to produce.

Depending on the construction of the panel, it can be assembled and finished either on or in the basic structure of the wall or completed as a separate unit and then installed. For large areas the former is usually necessary, while small panels can be finished before installation. In many instances the metal lath of the wall can be used as a base, the mural completed in place, and the areas around the design finished by a plasterer. Both movable and fixed wall panels, similar to stained-glass windows but lighted from the rear, can be constructed by several methods. Leading strips or epoxy cement can be used to hold the slabs together. Fixed panels should be planned as an integral part of the building by the architect, and access to the back of the panel for lighting control must be provided. To illuminate movable panels, a shallow light box is constructed. Fluorescent bulbs are the most practical because of the comparatively shallow space they require. A reflective white background should be used behind the lights to distribute the light evenly over the entire panel.

Dee Church, a designer from Arizona, has developed a unique technique that she calls *mazdalith* (lighted stone). It is a much freer technique than those described above: the slabs can be of different thicknesses, and nodules and crystals can even be used. The only requirement is that the materials be relatively translucent in order to transmit light and color. The technique is comparatively simple. A rigid background of heavy, transparent plexiglass is used, on which the materials are attached, piece by piece, with transparent epoxy. Although the pieces should fit closely together, there is no need to make perfect joints. After the epoxy has dried to maximum hardness and strength, the joints are filled with a white ceramic grout. The grout is colored with a fabric dye, such as Rit or Tintex, to blend with the adjacent pieces. The joints are practically invisible when the panel is viewed as a whole: although the grout is not translucent, it is applied in very narrow interstices and shows only as a thin outline. After the grout has set, a grout hardener is applied. When the entire panel becomes stable, it is cleaned and polished by hand with fine steel wool and cerium or tin oxide. A light coating of wax is applied and buffed to complete the finish. The effect of the work is created by both transmitted and reflected light. Wall panels and table tops can also be made with similar materials and techniques, although they are unlighted from the rear (5-52).

Pictorial Compositions

Pictures composed of gem materials have a long history: the techniques became highly developed in Roman Italy and flourished during the Renaissance and into the modern period. Various techniques are employed to create a flat design or picture. *Intarsia* and *marquetry* primarily refer to multicolored pictorial woodwork, while *parquetry* denotes a geometric pattern laid in a floor, wall, or other large area. *Mosaic* designates a technique in which small pieces of material are embedded in cement or adhesive to form a pictorial or abstract design. The pieces can be loosely fitted together, allowing the cement to show, or so small (1mm to 2mm) and fitted so precisely that the appearance of an unbroken surface is created. These terms have become confusingly interchangeable as the techniques have broadened in range to include materials such as wood, glass, and stone. Fine distinctions are seldom drawn: "intarsia," in lapidary, has come to mean any work of a pictorial nature, regardless of technique; "inlay" tends to be used for the entire field of stone embedment.

Making pictures with gem materials has had great attraction for lapidaries throughout history. Some technically astonishing works have been produced, but no significant artwork exists in this medium. The reason may lie in the fact that other more direct media are far more suitable for pictorial concepts. Too many lapidary-artists try to display technical virtuosity rather than communicate significant artistic ideas. Most such pictures are copies of famous paintings, whose tonal effects the lapidary tries to imitate. Each medium has its own sphere, dictated by the unique qualities of its materials. It is bad aesthetics to force one into the realm of another. This does not exclude the possibility of using gem materials to make pictures that do not attempt painted effects, particularly in abstract compositions. This field remains to be investigated by contemporary artists.

5-52. *Collage*, stone wall panel, 4' high, 2' wide, made by Dee Church.

Shop Tools

Some items used in the jewelry shop can be made by the lapidary-jeweler himself with gem materials. They are superior to the commercial metal equivalents, which makes producing them a worthwhile project.

A jeweler's anvil or surface plate can be made of a sawed block of jade that is heavy enough to stay in place on the bench when struck. It is better in all respects than the standard steel anvil: it does not mar nor lose its polish easily and thus imparts a smooth surface to metal worked on it. If the block is 1 1/2″ thick or more, it will not break under the heaviest blows. The other dimensions are relative: any convenient size for a work surface. Top edges should be slightly beveled to prevent damage. Low-grade, inexpensive jade can be used if the block is sound.

A slab of jade or agate also makes an excellent mixing surface for adhesives. Certain kinds of jasper make excellent sharpening stones. An agate mortar and pestle can be used to grind enamels and diamond abrasive and to powder fluxes. The very finest burnishers and prong pushers for setting gemstones can be made of jade and agate. The general shapes of steel tools can be followed, but agate tools should be slightly heavier to prevent chipping or breaking under pressure (5-53). Such tools will not become dull or scratched when used on gold or silver, and they will leave a highly polished finish on the metal—ideal for burnishing out slip scratches in engraving. A combination burnisher and prong pusher can be made of jade, ivory, and silver (5-54).

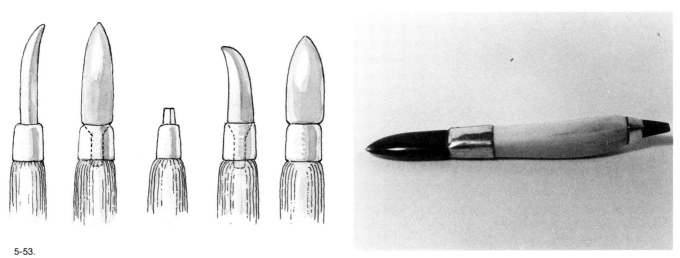

5-53.

5-54.

6. Design

It is both surprising and disappointing to discover how little concern most lapidaries have for design quality. There appears to be a general lack of understanding of what constitutes good design and how important it is in the creation of outstanding work. This is the fundamental reason why lapidary has so little standing as an artistic medium. The factors that created and perpetuated this situation are discussed in the preface. To correct the situation, it is important to understand what design means, its principles and values, and how important it is to the lapidary.

Design, as applied to any art object, is not merely an embellishment—an appealing surface addition. In the broadest and most accurate sense it is the arrangement of all the components to produce a specific aesthetic effect; it is how the work is conceived and constructed. It involves all stages of its creation from beginning to end. It includes the selection of materials and the manner in which they are combined. Even technique is an element of design: it is impossible to draw a line between design and craftsmanship; they are inevitably linked together. The technique must be appropriate to the structure, the function of the object, the materials, and the artistic idea. As for the importance of design to the lapidary: the question is answered in the definition. It is the most important concern in any art object, regardless of the medium. It is the essence of the work, the voice with which it speaks, the expression of the creator's personality. No amount of technical perfection can overcome the effect of a weak, ill-conceived design.

The objectives that you seek in your work determine how seriously you respond to the idea that design is all-important. Many people with a high degree of mechanical interest and ability are attracted to lapidary work because it offers a technical challenge. Other

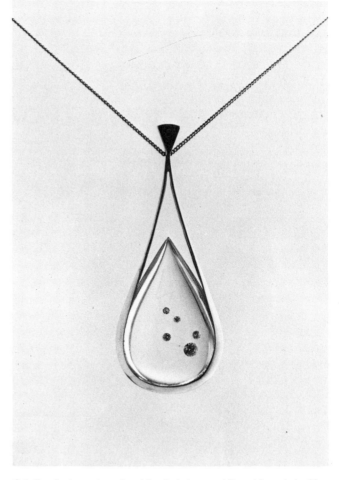

6-1. Pendant, quartz, colored faceted stones, white gold, made by Margaret de Patta, stones by Francis J. Sperisen.

people are interested in the geology and mineralogy of the materials. Although the beauty of the materials undoubtedly acts as an incentive for their work, it is not their predominant concern. They may be content to strive for technical excellence and mechanical perfection; they may be satisfied with recognition in exhibitions sponsored by lapidary organizations, in which judgment is based on traditional rules, standards, and ideas, with little emphasis on creativity. On the other hand, many other people have a consuming interest in the aesthetic qualities of rocks and minerals. Their fascination with lapidary work stems from an incipient urge to bring to light the beauty that lies hidden in the rough stone. They want to go further, to create something of artistic value from these minerals. They become concerned with creativity and the problems of design.

If you fall into this category, you may wish to enlarge your horizons by participating in the field of contemporary crafts. Exhibitions, sponsored by prestigious museums and galleries, place the utmost emphasis on new ideas and fresh creative approaches. If you want to enter this highly competitive arena, you should arm yourself with superior design knowledge and ability.

It is somewhat discouraging that no provision is made in this kind of exhibition for lapidary work per se and that there is general ignorance of and possibly some prejudice, conscious or unconscious, against the medium. But this should act as a challenge and an incentive rather than as a discouragement. Exceptional design, superior craftsmanship, and striking originality can overcome this handicap. If enough good designer-craftsmen turn to lapidary and enter their work in these competitive exhibitions, the impact will change this apathetic attitude. Sheer excellence in design can overcome all odds.

But what constitutes creative excellence? It may be possible to define design, but *good* design is more difficult. An answer that involves specific examples is bound to be subjective, based to a large degree on the personal tastes and preferences of the viewer. Equally qualified judges often have conflicting reactions to the same work: one may reject it; another may give it a prize! In spite of this difficulty some generally accepted broad standards can be applied. One can say that the excellence of a design depends on how well the parts are coordinated into an effective whole. There is a feeling of inevitability in any outstanding design, a feeling that nothing could be changed in any way without damaging the total effect. There must also be a quality of uniqueness, of originality, for the work to attract atten-

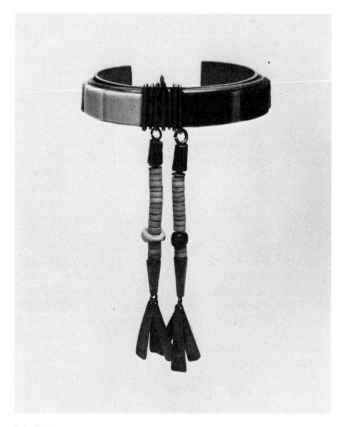

6-2. Eskimo bracelet, silver, ironwood, ivory, coral, shell, made by Jerry Norton.

6-3. Necklace, ivory, baleen.

tion and hold interest. If the concept of a design, its elements, and the way they are treated and combined have been seen in many other works, it becomes a commonplace statement. It adds nothing to one's aesthetic experience. To have real social significance, a design must be imbued with a feeling of newness, timeliness, an awareness of present-day cultural values. The fact that modern culture presents a picture of unprecedented complexity and disunity makes this a difficult requirement for the contemporary designer to fulfill. There are countless aesthetic contradictions and conflicts, popular movements of regression to primitivism, naturalism, superrealism, art nouveau, and the nostalgia of other periods in the past. This vast confusion and uncertainty have increased the numbers of charlatans and poseurs. Any eccentricity or absurdity is almost certain to receive serious consideration in some quarters, because all traditional values and standards have come into question. The individual artist must simply rely on his own evaluations, his own judgment of what is meaningful and what is nonsense, particularly in relation to the direction his own work should take. Future generations will judge present-day art as a whole on the basis of how well it expresses the spirit of this time, whatever that spirit may prove to be.

Given the importance of design and the existence of certain broad standards for measuring its quality, the next question—of particular importance to the beginner—is, how can a sense of design and an ability to design be developed? This is a very large and complex question, one to which no definitive answer can be given. In one sense good design cannot be taught. To have real significance, a design must bear the stamp of individuality. The projection of personality into one's work is never a conscious process; it grows out of complete understanding and control of the medium in which one works. Perfect assurance regarding the objective and how to attain it develops into a personal style, based on one's background and personality. Blindly following procedures that can be taught will never produce this result.

What can be taught are the unchanging fundamentals, inherent in all natural and man-made designs. A good teacher can help a student utilize these principles as a starting point for serious study and development. The best teachers can inspire their students: they have the ability to reveal the overwhelming but often hidden beauty of the visual world; to stimulate the student into an awareness of the myriad aspects of design in nature; to arouse his interest in the countless creative possibilities awaiting his discovery, especially those within himself. Even with the best guidance, however, the development of design ability depends on the initiative and effort of the student himself. Most successful designers, although they do not discount the importance of outside influences, agree that their development is largely the result of their own efforts, even while studying with a good teacher. This suggests that although instruction may be very helpful, it is by no means indispensable if a student can find adequate incentive elsewhere. Studying on one's own does require greater dedication and self-discipline than classroom study, where attendance is mandatory and the course is laid out systematically. But if you are determined, it is perfectly possible to dispense with formal instruction, as many top designers have done. The numerous good texts on design offer a practical substitute (see the bibliography).

6-4. Hopi silver bola tie, coral, jet, turquoise inlay, made by Preston Monongye.

Principles of Design

Any discussion of design, no matter how brief, should specify and define the elements on which all design is based. The fundamental elements are form, line, color, and texture. Shape, size, and mass are aspects of form.

Form is the most basic element. It can be either two-dimensional or three-dimensional. Most lapidary designs are three-dimensional—gemstones for jewelry, sculptural carvings, or hollow vessels—but some applications emphasize a flat, continuous surface—intarsia, inlay, and mosaic techniques for wall panels, tabletops, and windows are examples. The form of a three-dimensional object may be thought of as an object existing in space. Its total shape, or form, is what first attracts the eye, because it is the essence of its existence. For an art object to hold our interest its form must please, surprise, or shock the eye—some designs do all three. To have real meaning, the form must act as a framework for a unique aesthetic idea or feeling. Vacant spaces surrounding or contained within the object are equally as important as the solid form and must be carefully incorporated into the design. This effect is particularly evident in sculptures with hollow openings and in flat designs in which empty space becomes the background.

Line in one sense is an aspect of form, since it describes the shape by bounding it in space. This dependence is obvious in drawing: the draughtsman observes the visual boundaries of a three-dimensional object and sets them down as a line on a flat surface. Line refers to the pleasing arrangement of visible components. It does not consist exclusively of inscribed marks: it may be simply a boundary between different materials, colors, or textures or an imaginary line that the eye is led to follow through the design. Line can also be used to separate, join, or accent other elements of a design. It can become a decoration in itself: for instance, a single, continuous line that crosses itself many times to form an interesting arrangement of spaces in a pattern. By following the modulation of a form it can be used to emphasize its flow of movement. Multiple lines can create interesting areas of texture on the form's surface. Line is an extremely flexible tool for the designer.

Color is also an attribute of form. Although complete understanding and control of color are perhaps most vital to the painter and the decorator, a fine sense of color combination and arrangement is indispensable to most lapidary work. All materials have color, and lapidary materials cover a wide range of the spectrum (see appendix 1) with endless possible combinations. Selecting materials for specific color effects and combining them tastefully are immensely important in the creation

6-5. Ring, green tourmaline, white and yellow gold, made by Irena Brynner, stone by Francis J. Sperisen.

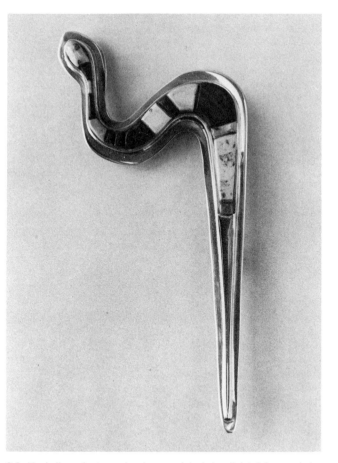

6-6. Hopi silver pin, turquoise, ironwood, lapis lazuli, jet inlay, made by Charles Loloma.

119

of an effective design. If metals are used, their colors must also be taken into account. They can be used either as a background or as accents for the colors of the stones.

Texture, like line and color, becomes a part of form in a well-conceived design. Although most lapidary involves highly polished surfaces, there are fascinating possibilities in varying textures for emphasis and variety, particularly with opaque solid-colored materials. Very subtle effects can be achieved by contrasting different textures in the same material. Textures can be imparted to gem materials by a variety of methods, depending on the characteristics of the particular stone. There are two kinds of texture: *visual* and *tactile*. Both are appropriate for lapidary work, depending on the function of the object, but visual texture is more common. It is usually translated by the viewer into the sensation of touch, whether it is actually touched or not. In viewing a rough texture, for instance, one is aware not only of how it looks but of how it would feel to the fingertips. A feeling for the tactile quality of texture is a valuable resource of the lapidary designer.

The principles by which the four basic elements are combined into perfectly coordinated designs derive from the same source. These abstract principles are inherent and visible throughout the natural environment. Rhythm, balance, unity, and variety have been analyzed and adopted by man to express aesthetic ideas in his own creative work.

Rhythm is a fundamental life force in all of nature. It can be perceived by all the senses; it can be found in all matter, animate or inaminate. The visual aspects of rhythm are expressed in art by means of *repetition* and *emphasis*, both of which are infinitely variable. Rhythm imparts movement to a design by flowing through it. Although it is customary to think of visual rhytym as undulating lines, it can be achieved by many other forms of repetition, such as sequential spots arranged in a repeating pattern.

Balance is the principle of equalizing the respective weights of different parts of a design to give a feeling of stability to the form. The simplest balance is *symmetrical:* two halves of a design are alike and equal in weight. A symmetrical design can be static and uninteresting unless the total form is unusual and exciting in some other way.

Asymmetrical balance is achieved by equalizing unlike shapes, colors, or texture. Relative placement in terms of the object's center of gravity helps to accomplish it: placing a small mass farther from this center than a larger mass on the opposite side, for example.

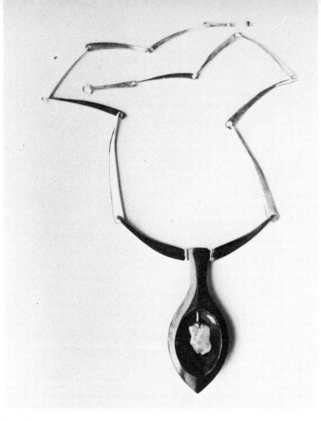

6-7. Pendant necklace, black jade, Mexican fire opal, 14K gold.

6-8. *Leo Crustacean*, microrelief, gold, silver, copper, lapis lazuli, 1 1/2" high, 1" wide, made by Harold O'Connor.

120

The centerline acts as a fulcrum, just as in the beam of a balance scale. Balance also results from many more subtle methods of maneuvering the elements of line, form, color, and texture in relationship to each other in order to create a feeling of gravitational stability.

The principle of *unity* draws all the elements and parts of a design together into a single form. The use of related materials or the repetition of a color, shape, or texture motif throughout the design imparts a feeling of unity.

Variety is a means of creating animation and excitement. It can be achieved by varying the sizes of the forms, the values and intensities of the colors, the width and spacing of the lines, or the smoothness and roughness of the textures. It is not the opposite of unity: elements expressing variety must have a unity of their own.

The above definitions of design elements and principles of organization are narrow simplifications. They merely provide an introduction, a groundwork, for further study and investigation. Definitions from other sources vary somewhat in what they include and emphasize, since each writer, instructor, student, and artist has a slightly different approach to design. Unlike science, no definitive laws, rules, or principles can be applied to any art form. Science is exact, predictable, and impersonal; art is inexact, unpredictable, and highly personal. At the same time the basic elements and principles do exist, although they are difficult to formulate exactly. An understanding of them is of great importance to the designer, even though each designer may understand and apply them differently to create individually unique results according to his personal vision.

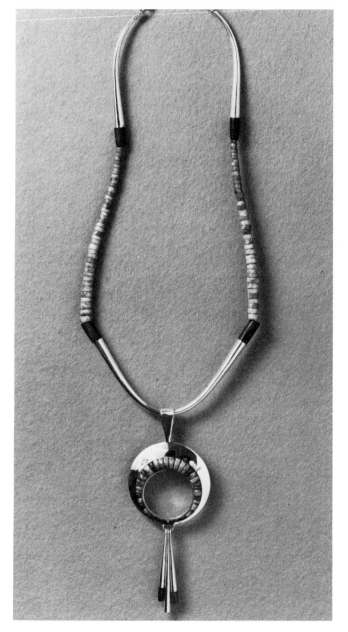

6-9. Hopi necklace, silver, turquoise, ironwood, coral, lapis lazuli, made by Charles Loloma.

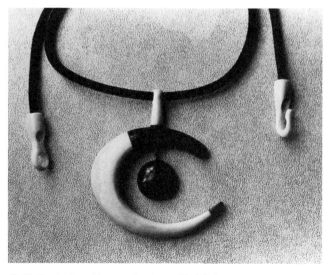

6-10. Pendant necklace, walrus ivory, black jade.

The greatest asset of the creative designer is his ability to *see*. This ability has to be developed: it is not a natural talent. It is based on experience, concentration, and a knowledge of what to look for. The process of seeing in this sense is not merely optical: it includes an analysis of what is seen in terms of its aesthetic significance. To develop this ability, one must learn to look critically at every kind of man-made object. It is important to see as wide a variety of work as possible: the same principles are involved in every art and craft. One should analyze each piece, find the underlying principles and elements of design, assess its design quality, and justify one's opinion. A good design is seldom obvious, but a discerning eye can detect the components. Critical ability directly affects one's own work for the better.

Still more effective is to study the design of natural forms. It is doubtful that the mind of man can invent a form that is not found somewhere in the macrocosm or microcosm of nature, an inexhaustible source of design material. The aerial viewpoint reveals patterns that are invisible at ground level; microphotographs offer strangely beautiful and stimulating images. The shapes in rocks, rock formations, and mineral crystals; plant stems, leaves, flowers, seeds; skeletons of animals; larva, pupa, and adult insect stages; decaying surfaces of rocks, wood, bones; scaling paint and corroding metals—everything is a potential source of design ideas. Nothing should be copied literally but used as a takeoff point for flights of invention. Concentrating on seeing form provides a solid fund of visual material on which to draw, consciously and unconsciously, in designing. If one learns to practice it habitually, it will heighten one's powers of observation and increase one's awareness of the visual world.

How to approach a problem in design depends a great deal on temperament. Designers can be roughly divided into two types: spontaneous and deliberate (although every good designer is a bit of both). The spontaneous ones are inclined to evolve the design as they work, either in the final material or in an intermediate material such as the wax used for lost-wax casting in metal; the deliberate ones generally make sketches to clarify the design before committing it to either the final or the intermediate material. Great spontaneity may go into the preliminary sketch; a lot of deliberation may be involved in developing and perfecting the spontaneous idea conceived in the material itself. A note of warning to the student: beware of a teacher who is dogmatic about which approach to use. One fairly well-known instructor in the lost-wax-casting technique expels any student from his class who dares to make a preliminary design! Each method is valid; the choice is a highly personal one that should be decided by the individual after experimenting with each.

Another consideration is that some materials are better suited to one method than to the other. Clay and wax are suitable for spontaneous sculpture; direct carving requires a more deliberate method. Lost-wax casting is convenient for spontaneous effects—although not limited to them—while construction in the metal itself makes careful preplanning almost mandatory. This condition is even more true of lapidary materials: because of their resistant nature, their hardness and complete lack of malleability, they demand a perfectly visualized design before work is actually begun. It is impossible to start carving with only a hazy idea of the final form in the hope that a successful design will evolve spontaneously. The material must be approached with a purpose rather than experimentally. This is not just an opinion; it is a rigid requirement of the material itself. More often than not it is necessary to work out a design on paper. In some cases, particularly for sculpture, it is advisable to draw views from several angles or even to carve a model in a soft material such as wax in order to crystallize a three-dimensional image of the finished form. Some spontaneous designers resist a material that requires such patient preplanning, but many find adequate freedom for intuitive creation in the preliminary sketches or models once they begin to understand and appreciate the characteristics of the new medium.

6-11. Hopi ring, silver, turquoise, coral, made by Louis Lomay.

Besides the necessity of preplanning the form some stones have unusual physical characteristics that must be taken into account in designing shapes. Stones that display optical phenomena such as chatoyancy and asterism (1-8) must be designed and oriented so that their unusual qualities are shown to best advantage. In the case of faceting rough the unique light-refraction and -dispersion characteristics of each particular material must be considered to obtain the greatest degree of brilliance. In some of the cryptocrystalline materials the arrangement of lines and colors may dictate or strongly influence the design. This is particularly true of banded and fortification agates, orbicular and reticulated jaspers, and other highly patterned stones. Some of the agates and jaspers are so beautiful and interesting in themselves that it is difficult to incorporate them in a successful design. The so-called fancy-colored jaspers; moss, plume, fern, flower, and landscape agates; and petrified wood of the picture-wood variety have such intriguing, eye-catching patterns and effects that the designer may feel dominated by this kind of material and find it impossible to create a forceful personal expression. The best way to use such stones is to treat them as simply as possible. The designer should not try to compete with a design or picture in the stone but should present it in as favorable and tasteful a setting as possible. Such materials are very beautiful but not as easy to incorporate in original designs as are stones that are less intrinsically interesting.

If the sculptural form of the object is to provide the focus of attention, the shape of the piece in the rough may suggest a design. This may also be true of inclusions or areas of color variation. Chinese and Japanese designers are famous for their ability to utilize effects or even defects in the material to enhance their designs. Chinese jade carvers habitually began their work by studying the material with intense concentration, often over a long period of time, until "the form that is in the stone" revealed itself. The mental image would become so clear that the carving could proceed with assurance. Eskimo carvers follow the same mystical approach. They believe that there is an identity, an inherent spirit, in each piece of material, waiting to be released by a human hand. It may not be possible to develop such certitude and such reverence for materials in this day and culture. But every sensitive designer is sometimes aware of a power that moves his hand in the right direction without his volition. Closer rapport with this mysterious creative force is what all artists are unconsciously seeking.

Contemporary Lapidary Design

Although creative lapidary work has been almost completely ignored by contemporary designer-craftsmen, there are some indications that the situation is changing. The change of attitude can be attributed almost completely, though obliquely, to the phenomenal upsurge of public interest in Indian jewelry. Only the Indian jewelers have produced significant lapidary work in this century. In this comparatively short period of time since the beginning of their craft the Zuni Indians have risen to a high plateau of excellence in both design and technique. Most other Indian tribes have not placed such emphasis on lapidary skill, relying on dealers and traders for their stones.

Until comparatively recently Indian jewelry, like other Indian art forms, has remained by tradition a tribal rather than a personal form of expression. But several Indian craftsmen are now working in highly individualistic,

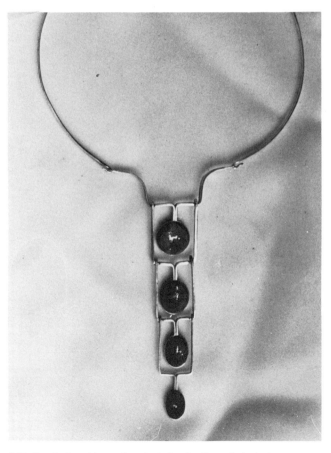

6-12. Pendant necklace, silver, lapis lazuli with pyrite inclusions.

123

nontraditional styles. Their work is thoroughly contemporary in its appeal but also unmistakably Indian in flavor. The widespread interest in Indian jewelry, which in the last few years has almost become a national fad, has focused attention on these exceptional craftsmen. Today their work is admired and sought after by discriminating patrons, not exclusively because of its Indian origin but also because it is significant contemporary expression. The success of the Indian lapidary has also aroused the interest of non-Indian jewelers, some of whom have begun to see the possibilities and advantages of working with gemstone materials. Under this influence they are developing lapidary skills appropriate to their own styles. Successful adaptations of the colorful materials of Indian jewelry, such as turquoise, coral, marine shells, tortoiseshell, and jet, have expanded to include malachite, chrysocolla, lapis lazuli, ivory, horn, and other materials. This development may be the beginning of a trend toward more colorful jewelry, as in the art-nouveau period a century ago.

Among the Indian craftsmen who are prominent in this movement, Charles Loloma, a Hopi from Hotevilla, Second Mesa, Arizona, is the most influential. His strikingly original work, which is highly personal in style although rooted in Hopi tradition, has gained national and international recognition (6-6, 6-9, and 6-13). Most Indian and non-Indian lapidaries in the Southwest have been inspired by Loloma. Roger Tsabetsaye, a Zuni from Zuni, New Mexico, has done outstanding metal- and stonework and combinations of the two. His work is also both highly individualistic and Indian in feeling (4-26, C-1, and C-17). Louis Mojica, a Hopi from Albuquerque, New Mexico, although quite young, expresses many influences other than those of his ancestral tradition. His work is superb in both feeling and technique and successfully incorporates traditional design motifs and a personal, contemporary approach (5-15, C-15, and C-16). Preston Monongye, a Hopi (6-4); Louis Lomay (Lomayesva), Hopi (6-11); and Kenny Begay, a Navajo (4-17), should be mentioned both for the high degree of excellence of their work and for the fact that it clearly shows a trend toward more personal forms of expression.

Several non-Indian jewelers in the Southwest have been greatly influenced by these contemporary Indian designers. Successful work of any kind will always attract imitators (witness the flood of spurious Indian jewelry), but the craftsmen mentioned below do not fall into that category. Although their work derives from Indian styles and techniques, they are seriously working toward a realization of their own potentialities for personal expression. Eveli (she uses only her first name)

is a fine jewelry craftsman with a European background who now works in Santa Fe, New Mexico. She is perhaps the most original of the jewelers influenced by Indian work. Her work is extremely varied and imaginative in design, and much of it shows more personal expression than the work of many other non-Indian craftsmen (C-9 and C-14). Steve Ballard, of Albuquerque, New Mexico, is one of the better and more successful young jewelers working in his idiom (C-4 and C-23). Curt Pfeffer, of Sedona, Arizona, is also producing some excellent work based on the colorful materials of Indian jewelry (C-6 and C-8).

None of these craftsmen, Indian or non-Indian, has produced equally fine work with the harder, more durable stones. This may be partly due to demand: because of the immense interest in the colorful Indian materials there is not much incentive to investigate other possibilities. All of the Indian materials are less than 6 in hardness, comparatively easily worked with simple equipment and carved with hand tools. The few designs incorporating harder materials are disappointing due to a lack of training and experience. But this situation can easily change: it requires only one talented craftsman with the curiosity and imagination to investigate the possibilities of other materials and other approaches.

Native craftsmen outside the Southwest have also produced lapidary work of admirable quality in recent years. In southeast Alaska some of the Tlingits and Haidas have done remarkable carvings in steatite and serpentine (4-34). The same is true of a rather large

6-13. Hopi silver bracelet, turquoise, coral, lapis lazuli, ironwood inlay, made by Charles Loloma.

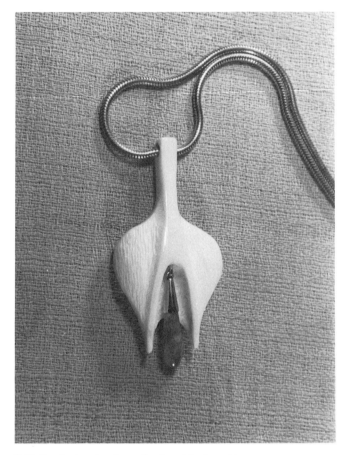

6-14. Pendant, walrus ivory, fossil-seal tooth, gold.

number of Eskimos in the far North, who have learned to work native jade, ivory, baleen, and caribou hoof with modern equipment (4-3, 4-28, 4-30, 4-35, 5-7, 5-8, and 6-2). Other craftsmen of different tribes have produced excellent carvings in various stone materials. The Indian Arts and Crafts Board and the Institute of American Indian Art, operated by the federal government, are responsible for training programs that have developed native talent in several areas of the country.

It is unfortunate that space does not permit a more complete discussion of the craftsmen who are working creatively with lapidary techniques. Although great effort has been made to locate and contact everyone who should be included in this book, some qualified individuals have undoubtedly been omitted. The author wishes to express his regrets for such unintentional omissions.

Appendix 1.
Hardness and Color of Gem Materials

diamond	10	colorless, yellow, red, blue, gray, black
corundum	9	black, all colors
ruby		red
sapphire		blue
chrysoberyl	8	yellow to green to gray
alexandrite		green by day, red by artificial light
oriental cat's-eye		gray to green
spinel	8	red, lavender, blue, green, brown, black
topaz	8	colorless, yellow, pink, bluish, greenish
phenacite	7.5–8	white, colorless
andalusite	7.5	flesh red, red
euclase	7.5	pale green or blue to white
zircon	7.5	gray, green, yellow, red (blue and colorless when treated)
uvarovite	7.5	emerald green
tourmaline	7–7.5	black, green, yellow, blue, red, colorless
achroite		colorless
indicolite		blue
rubellite		red
beryl	7–7.5	green, greenish blue, pink, yellow
emerald		deep green
aquamarine		greenish blue
cordierite	7–7.5	blue, smoky blue, greenish blue
garnet	6.5–7.5	red, green, yellow
almandine		reddish, purplish, brownish
andradite		brown, bright green (demantoid)
grossularite		colorless, white, green, yellow, brown, red
pyrope		bright red to brownish red
rhodolite		pale reddish purple
spessartite		orange, dark red, brownish red
dumortierite	7	deep blue
jadeite	7	white, yellow, orange, blue, green, violet, brown
quartz	7	all colors, black, white
rock crystal		colorless
citrine		yellow
smoky quartz		gray
amethyst		lavender to purple
chalcedony		white, yellow, brown
chrysoprase		emerald to yellow-green
agate		all colors
jasper		all colors

chert		dull colors, black, white
flint		dull colors, black, white
danburite	7	deep blue
spodumene	6.5–7	white
kunzite		lavender pink
hiddenite		emerald green
olivine	6.5–7	olive to grayish green, brown
chrysolite		light golden yellow
peridot		deep yellow-green
axinite	6.5–7	brown, gray, green, yellow
epidote	6–7	yellowish to blackish green, gray
cassiterite	6–7	brown to black, rarely yellow to white
cyanite	5–7	blue, white, gray, green
idocrase	6.5	green, brown, yellow, blue, red
prehnite	6–6.5	apple green, gray, white
nephrite	6–6.5	green, white, black, gray, yellowish, bluish, brown, red
marcasite	6–6.5	pale yellow to almost white
pyrite	6–6.5	pale brass yellow, silvery
rutile	6–6.5	yellow, reddish brown to black
rhodonite	6–6.5	rose red, pink, brown
zoisite	6–6.5	gray, yellow-brown, greenish gray, apple green
opal	5.5–6.5	all colors, play of spectrum colors in precious opal
hematite	5.5–6.5	steel gray to iron black
feldspar	6	many colors
sunstone		reddish with gold schiller
moonstone		gray, pink, brownish, bluish, yellowish, greenish
amazonite		green, blue with silvery chatoyancy
peristerite		flesh color with blue chatoyancy
labradorite		gray with chatoyant play of colors
bytownite		yellow
nephelite	5.5–6	colorless, gray, greenish, reddish
beryllonite	5.5–6	colorless, white
sodalite	5.5–6	deep violet-blue, white, gray, green
thomsonite	5–5.5	white, pink, green, brown
datolite	5–5.5	colorless, pale green, yellow
dioptase.	5	emerald green
pectolite	5	colorless, white, gray
smithsonite	5	brown, green, blue
odontolite	5	blue, blue-green, green
apatite	5	green, blue, violet, yellow, pink
serpentine	2.5–5	olive, black, green, yellow-green, blue-green, white
rhodochrosite	3.5–4.5	rose red, dark red, brown
azurite	3.5–4	intense, deep azure blue
malachite	3.5–4	bright banded green
aragonite	3.5–4	colorless, white, variously tinted
calcite	3.5–4	colorless, white, variously tinted
satin spar		colorless, white, variously tinted
Iceland spar		colorless, white, variously tinted
coral	3.5–4	red, orange, pink, white, black
sphalerite	3.5–4	dark brown to coal black
ivory	3.5–4	yellowish white (brown, black, blue, orange when fossilized)

howlite	3.5	white
chrysocolla	2–4	blue-green to bright blue
amber	2–2.5	red, yellow, orange
copal	2–2.5	yellow
gypsum	2	colorless, white, gray
alabaster	2	colorless, white, gray
steatite	1	apple green, gray, white, pink, brown, yellow
talc	1	gray, white, yellowish
wood	1–4	many colors and patterns

Note: Wood is not strictly a lapidary material, but it is often used in the same manner as the softer gem materials by lapidaries and jewelers. Only the harder woods are practical for this purpose: ebony and rosewood are the most common, although there are a number of other exotic woods that are even harder and more durable.

Appendix 2.
Speed Tables and Formulas

Revolutions per minute (r.p.m.) with various pulley combinations using a 1,725 r.p.m. motor

diameter of motor pulley

diameter of pulley on machine in inches

	1¼	1½	1¾	2	2¼	2½	3	4	5	6½	8	10	12
1¼	1725	1435	1230	1075	950	850	715	540	430	330	265	215	175
1½	2075	1725	1475	1290	1140	1030	850	645	515	395	320	265	215
1	2400	2000	1725	1500	1340	1200	1000	750	600	460	375	315	250
2	2775	2290	1970	1725	1530	1375	1145	850	685	530	430	345	285
2¼	3100	2580	2200	1930	1725	1550	1290	965	775	595	485	385	325
2½	2450	2870	2460	2150	1900	1725	1435	1075	850	660	540	430	335
3	4140	3450	2950	2580	2290	2070	1725	1290	1070	800	615	515	430
4	5500	4575	3950	3450	3060	2775	2295	1725	1375	1060	860	700	575
5	6850	5750	4920	4300	3825	3450	2865	2150	1725	1325	1075	860	715
5½	8950	7475	6400	5600	4975	4480	3730	2790	2240	1725	1400	1120	930

Required r.p.m. for speeds in surface feet per minute (s.f.m.) with various wheel and blade diameters

approximate peripheral speeds in feet per minute

diameter in inches	1000	2000	3000	4000	5000	6000	7000	8000
				r.p.m. required				
1	3820	7640	11460	15280	19100	22920	26740	30560
2	1910	3820	5730	7640	9550	11460	13340	15280
3	1275	2550	3820	5095	6370	7640	8915	10190
4	955	1910	2865	3820	4775	5730	6685	7640
6	635	1275	1910	2550	3185	3820	4455	5095
8	475	955	1430	1910	2385	2865	3340	3820
10	380	765	1145	1530	1910	2290	2675	3055
12	320	635	955	1275	1590	1910	2230	2545
14	275	545	820	1090	1365	1635	1910	2185
16	240	475	715	955	1195	1430	1670	1910
18	210	425	635	850	1060	1275	1485	1700
20	190	380	575	765	955	1145	1336	1530
24	160	320	475	635	795	955	1115	1275
30	125	255	380	510	635	765	890	1020

The above tables are accurate enough for practical purposes, but if other sizes and speeds are involved, the following formulas can be used for calculation.

Required: speed of driven pulley
Multiply the diameter of the driving pulley by its speed in r.p.m. and divide the product by the diameter of the driven pulley. Example: $\frac{2 \times 1725}{4}$ = 862, approximate r.p.m. of machine pulley.

Required: diameter of driven pulley
Multiply the diameter of the driving pulley by its speed in r.p.m. and divide by the required speed of the driven pulley. Example: $\frac{2 \times 1725}{850}$ = 4, diameter of driven pulley.

Required: diameter of driving pulley
Multiply the diameter of the driven pulley by its speed in r.p.m. and divide by the speed of the driving pulley. Example: $\frac{4 \times 850}{1725}$ = 2, diameter of driving pulley.

Required: speed of driving pulley
Multiply the diameter of the driven pulley by its speed in r.p.m. and divide by the diameter of the driving pulley. Example: $\frac{4 \times 850}{2}$ = 1725, speed of driving pulley.

Required: s.f.m. of wheel
Multiply r.p.m. by π (3.14), multiply the result by the diameter of the wheel, and divide by 12. Example: 850 × 3.14 × 8 ÷ 12 = 1780, speed of wheel.

Appendix 3.
Sources of Supply

General Equipment

Highland Park Manufacturing
12600 Chadron Ave.
Hawthorne, Calif. 90250

Covington Engineering Corp.
112 First Street
Redland, Calif. 92373

Alta Industries
918 W. Norwich Ave.
Fresno, Calif. 93705

Crown Manufacturing Co.
(steel tubing, steel core drills)
910 W. Vallecitos Blvd.
San Marcos, Calif. 92069

Lortone Division,
Carborundum Co.
2856 Northwest Market St.
Seattle, Wash. 98107

Great Western Equipment Co.
3444 Main Street
Chula Vista, Calif. 92011

The Ducketts
P.O. Box 969
Medford, Oregon 97501

Hillquist
1545 N.W. 49th St.
Seattle, Wash. 98107

Lapidary Hobbycrafts
911 West 9 Mile Rd.
Ferndale, Mich. 48220

Rock's Lapidary Equipment
P.O. Box 10075
San Antonio, Tx. 78210

A. D. McBurney
1610 Victory Blvd.
Glendale, Calif. 91201

Diamond Tools and Equipment

Ran-Co Lapidary Products
19015 Parthenia St.
Northridge, Calif. 91324

Gem-Tec Diamond Tool Co.
7310 Melrose St.
Buena Park, Calif. 90620

Metro Diamond Drill Co.
(drills)
845 Masselin Ave.
Los Angeles, Calif. 90036

Crystalite Corp.
13449 Beach Ave.
Marina del Rey, Calif. 90291

Diamond-Pro, Unlimited
(carving tools, drills)
P.O. Box 25
Monterey Park, Calif. 91754

Diamond Pacific
25647 W. Main St.
Barstow, Calif. 92311

Starlite Industries
(core drills)
1111 Lancaster Ave.
Rosemont, Pa. 19010

Faceting Equipment

Earth Treasures Division,
Dick Blick Co.
P.O. Box 1267
Galesburg, Ill. 61401

Lee Lapidaries
3425 West 117th St.
Cleveland, Ohio 44111

MDR Manufacturing Co., Inc.
2686 S. LaCienega Blvd.
Los Angeles, Calif. 90034

Carving Machines

Precise Products,
Power Tool Division,
Rockwell International
3715 Blue River Road
Racine, Wisc. 53401

Dremel Mfg. Division,
Emerson Electric Co.
P.O. Box 518
Racine, Wisc. 53408

Paul H. Gesswein & Co.
235 Park Ave. South
New York, N.Y. 10003

Chicago Wheel & Mfg. Co.
1101 W. Monroe St.
Chicago, Ill. 60607

Tumblers

Vibra Tek
2807 North Prospect St.
Colorado Springs, Colo. 80907

Lortone Division,
Carborundum Co.
2856 Northwest Market St.
Seattle, Wash. 98107

Jewelry Tools and Equipment

Paul H. Gesswein & Co.
235 Park Ave. South
New York, N.Y. 10003

Friedheim Tool Supply Co.
412 West Sixth St.
Los Angeles, Calif. 90014

Allcraft Tool & Supply Co., Inc.
215 Park Ave.
Hicksville, N.Y. 11801

Swest Smelting & Refining Co.
10803 Composite Drive
Dallas, Tx. 75220

Gem Materials

Goodnow Gems U.S.A.
5740 Canyon Drive
Amarillo, Tx. 79109

Minerals and Gems
P.O. Box 5351
Albany, New York 12205

International Import Co.
P.O. Box 747
Stone Mountain, Ga. 30083

Bergsten Jade Co.
P.O. Box 2381
Castro Valley, Calif. 94546

Loex Jades, Limited
3182 Camosun St.
Vancouver, B.C., Canada VXR 3X1

Carico Lake Mining Co.
3318 Girard Blvd., N.E.
Albuquerque, N.M. 87110

Parser Mineral Corp.
P.O. Box 2076
Golden Hills, Danbury, Ct. 06810

Midwest Distributor (elephant ivory)
Box 2772 Station A
Champaign, Ill. 61820

Maruskiya's of Nome (fossil ivory)
Nome, Alaska 99762

Fire Mountain Gems
802 Mulholland Drive
Los Angeles, Calif. 90046

Glossary

amorphous having no crystalline structure.

aperture an opening in a carving that serves as part of the design.

arbor a shaft, or mandrel, on which rotary tools or wheels are mounted.

asterism a mineral property in which a star is formed on a polished domed surface by reflected light rays.

axis an imaginary line passing through the center of a stone or crystal.

azure to change the shape of a circular hole drilled in a piece of material.

backrest a plate, mounted on a post, that contains shallow depressions in which a lap stick is placed for faceting; a jamb peg.

bezel a band of metal surrounding and holding a stone in the mounting.

bond a substance that holds abrasive grains together in a grinding tool; the holding property of an adhesive.

bort industrial-diamond crystals or particles used in manufacturing diamond tools.

botryoidal grapelike in form, as the surface of a mineral.

bow drill a primitive tool used to drill very small holes.

boxwood a very hard, fine-grained wood used to make small polishing wheels and points.

burnisher a metal or stone hand tool that utilizes compression to close bezel settings and polish metal.

burr the cutting head of a steel or abrasive carving tool.

bushing a sleeve or collar used to adapt a wheel to an arbor that is smaller in diameter than the hole.

cabochon an unfaceted stone with a rounded top.

cameo a carving or engraving in material layered in two or more colors.

carbonado a tough, industrial-grade black diamond used in making drills and other tools.

carbuncle a garnet cut in cabochon form; any red stone cut as a large, heavy cabochon.

cast in place in lost-wax casting to enclose the gem material in the metal mold with the wax pattern and cast the metal with the stone in position.

chevet a type of carving or engraving in which the border is higher than the design.

chuck the adjustable attachment on the shaft of a drilling or carving machine used to hold rotary tools.

collet a type of holder, similar to a chuck, in which the shanks of small tools are mounted in a machine.

conchoidal shell-like or fanlike in shape, as a fracture in a mineral.

concretion a rounded mass of stone formed around a nucleus.

coolant a solution for cooling and lubricating the cutting action in a lapidary machine.

countersink to grind a small, concentric depression at the upper end of a drill hole.

Cratex trade name of a line of rubber-abrasive wheels and points.

crown the top of a gemstone.

cryptocrystalline formed of microscopic crystals.

crystalline formed of crystals large enough to be seen by the naked eye.

crystallography the scientific study of crystal structure.

dendrite a treelike pattern that appears in many gem materials.

dop to fasten a stone with wax to the end of a rod or stick for cutting and polishing; the rod that holds the stone in a faceting machine.

dress to smooth a grinding wheel or tool.

druse an encrustation of small crystals on the surface of a mineral.

encrust to embed a metal, usually fine gold, in lines engraved below the surface of a gem material.

etch to form a design on the surface of a gem material by corroding it with acid.

facet a flat plane on the surface of a natural crystal or on a cut gem.

feather a liquid-filled cavity with a featherlike configuration, seen in some translucent and transparent materials.

findings metal parts for wearing jewelry, such as earring backs, pin backs, or clasps.

fortification agate a type of agate with concentric bands that resemble an aerial view of a fortification—walls within walls.

geode a hollow nodule or concretion, often lined with agate and/or crystals.

girdle the narrow, slightly beveled plane ground on the periphery of a cabochon-type stone to facilitate mounting in a bezel.

glandular shaped like a gland; oval or kidney-shaped.

glyptic the carving or engraving of gemstones.

goniometer an instrument for measuring the interfacial angles of crystals.

grit, or **grain** abrasive particles used in lapidary processes.

inlay any of several techniques in which materials are embedded to form a design.

intaglio engraving in which the design is carved below the surface plane.

interfacial angle the angle formed by any two faces of a crystal.

iris a variety of quartz showing iridescence on fractured surfaces, sometimes in thin, translucent sections.

jamb peg a backrest used in faceting.

lap a plate or machine used to grind flat faces on gem materials.

lenticular shaped like a lens, as a double cabochon.

mammillary nipplelike in formation, as the surface of a mineral.

mandrel an arbor.

massive having no visible crystalline form.

matrix the mother rock in which a mineral is formed.

Mohs' scale a comparative scale of mineral hardness.

moss a formation in gem material resembling moss; originally thought to be silicified organic material but now proved to be of mineral origin.

nodule a roughly rounded mass of mineral matter.

onyx black-and-white layered agate; colorless agate dyed black; alabaster; black marble.

orbicular having eyelike markings.

pavilion the entire back of a faceted stone.

peripheral speed surface speed of a rotating wheel or other rotary tool.

plasticene a type of modeling clay.

reamer a tool used to enlarge drill holes.

reniform shaped like a kidney.

reticulated having a pattern of netlike lines.

r.p.m. revolutions per minute, as of an arbor or spindle of a machine.

score to incise shallow grooves in the surface of a lap plate to hold a charge of diamond grit.

s.f.m., or **s.f.p.m.** Surface or peripheral speed in feet per minute of a wheel or other rotary tool.

shim a wedge used to secure a piece of material in a saw vise.

silicon carbide man-made corundum, used as an abrasive.

silk a chatoyant optical effect found in corundum materials.

sintered fused into a bond by heat-treating, as with some diamond tools.

slurry a fluid mixture of grit and water.

splendent gleaming or lustrous in surface reflection.

stone gauge an instrument for checking angles in faceting.

stylus a sharp point used to inscribe lines on the surface of a gem material.

table the flat top surface of a faceted stone or of a similar type of cut.

template a pattern for marking the outline of a cut on a stone and for checking the accuracy of the outline.

wheel a lapidary grindstone.

Bibliography

Design

Best-Mangard, Adolfo, *A Method for Design*, Knopf, New York, 1926.

Boas, Franz, *Primitive Art*, Dover, New York, 1955.

Bossert, Helmuth T., *Decorative Arts of Asia and Egypt*, Praeger, New York, 1956.

——, *Folk Art of Europe*, Praeger, New York, 1953.

——, *Folk Art of Primitive Peoples*, Praeger, New York, 1953.

Christensen, Erwin O., *Index of American Design*, National Gallery of Art, Macmillan, New York, 1950.

Anderson, Donald M., *Elements of Design*, Holt, Rinehart, and Winston, New York, 1963.

Berlin, Marjorie Elliott, *Design Through Discovery*, Holt, Rinehart, and Winston, New York, 1963.

Moseley, Spencer, Pauline Johnson, and Hazel Koenig, *Crafts Design*, Wadsworth, Belmont, Ca., 1962.

Douglas, Frederick Huntington and Rene D'Harnoncourt, *Indian Art of the United States*, Museum of Modern Art, New York, 1941.

Kepes, Gyorgy, *Language of Vision*, Paul Theobald, Chicago, 1941.

Lewis, Albert B., *Decorative Art of New Guinea*, Field Museum of Natural History, Chicago, 1925.

Linton, Ralph and Paul S. Wingart, *Arts of the South Seas*, Museum of Modern Art, New York, 1946.

Lipman, Jean, *American Folk Art*, Pantheon, New York, 1948.

Moholy-Nagy, *Vision in Motion*, Paul Theobald, Chicago, 1947.

Munsterberg, Hugo, *The Folk Arts of Japan*, Tuttle, Rutland, Vermont and Tokyo, 1958.

Poulik, Josef et. al., *Prehistoric Art*, Tudor, New York.

——, *Etruscan Art*, Philosophical Library, New York, 1954.

Trowell, Margaret, *African Design*, Praeger, New York, 1960.

Hald, Arthur, *Contemporary Swedish Design*, Nordick Rotogravyr, 1951.

Mineralogy

Rogers, Austin F., *Introduction to the Study of Rocks and Minerals* (3rd edition), McGraw-Hill, New York, 1937.

Dana, Edward S., *A Textbook of Mineralogy* (4th edition), Wiley, New York, 1951.

Pearl, Richard M., *Popular Gemmology*, Wiley, New York, 1848.

Ford, W. E., *A Textbook of Mineralogy* (4th edition), Wiley, New York, 1932.

Hurlbut, G. S., *Minerals and How to Study Them*, Wiley, New York, 1952.

Lapidary and Jewelry Techniques

Quick, L. and H. Leiper, *How to Cut and Polish Gemstones*, Chilton, Philadelphia, 1959.

Sperisen, Francis J., *The Art of the Lapidary* (2nd edition), Bruce, Milwaukee, 1961.

Sinkankas, John, *Gem Cutting* (2nd edition), Van Nostrand Reinhold, New York, 1962.

Pond, Forest W., *How to Make and Use Gem Cutting Tools*, Pond, Santa Ana, Ca.

Howard, J. Harry, *Revised Lapidary Handbook*, Howard, Greenville, S.C., 1946.

O'Connor, Harold, *New Directions in Goldsmithing*, Dunconnor, Calgary, Canada, 1975.

Bovin, Murray, *Jewelry Making for Schools, Tradesmen, Craftsmen*, Bovin, Forest Hills, N.Y.

Choate, Sharr, *Creative Casting*, Crown, New York, 1966.

von Neumann, Robert, *Design and Creation of Jewelry*, Chilton, Philadelphia, 1961.

Adair, John, *Navajo and Pueblo Silversmiths*, University of Oklahoma, 1945.

Brynner, Irena, *Modern Jewelry, Design and Technique*, Van Nostrand Reinhold, New York, 1968.

Linick, Leslie L., *Jeweler's Workshop Practices*, Paulson, Chicago, 1948.

Winebrenner, D. Kenneth, *Jewelry Making as an Art Expression*, International Textbook, Scranton, Pa., 1953.

Field Guides for Gem Hunters

Desert Gem Trails, Strong, Gembooks, Mentone, California

Field Guide to the Gems and Minerals of Mexico, Gembooks, Mentone, California

Eastern Gem Trails, Oles, Gembooks, Mentone, California

Midwest Gem Trails, Zeitner, Gembooks, Mentone, California

The Handbook of Jade, Hemrich, Gembooks, Mentone, California

Appalachian Mineral and Gem Trails, Zeitner, Lapidary Journal, San Diego, California

Southwest Mineral and Gem Trails, Zeitner, Lapidary Journal, San Diego, California

New Mexico Gem Trails, Simpson, Gem Guides Book Co., Whittier, California
Gem Trails of Arizona, Simpson, Gem Guides Book Co., Whittier, California
Gem Trails of Texas, Simpson, Gem Guides Book Co., Whittier, California
Rocks and Minerals of California, Brown and Allan, Naturegraph, Healdsburg, California
Arizona Rock Trails, Bitner, Bitner's, Phoenix, Arizona
Colorado Gem Trails and Mineral Guide, Pearl, Swallow Press, Chicago

California Gem Trails, Henry, Gordon's, Long Beach, California
Gem and Mineral Localities of Southeastern United States, Willman, Willman, Jacksonville, Alabama

Magazines
Gems and Minerals (monthly)
Lapidary Journal (monthly)
Rock and Gem (bimonthly)

Index